Controlling Crop

Pests and Diseases

Rosalyn Rappaport

Formerly Horticulturalist,
USAID Project Maraicher,
Nouakchott,
Mauritania

Formerly Horticulturalist,
National Irrigation Research Station,
Mazabuka,
Zambia

Strip cartoons by Robin Edmonds

ITDG Publishing
2004

This edition published in 2004 by
ITDG Publishing
Bourton Hall, Bourton-on-Dunsmore
Rugby, Warwickshire,
CV23 9QZ, UK

ISBN 1-85339-600-1

A CIP catalogue record for this book is available from
the British Library

First published by THE MACMILLAN PRESS LTD 1992
London and Basingstoke
Publication supported by the Technical Centre for Agriculture and Rural
Co-operation (CTA), Netherlands
Reprinted 1993

Manufacture coordinated in UK by Book-in-Hand Ltd
20 Shepherds Hill London N6 5AH

Contents

Preface

How to use this book

This handbook was written for the men and women of the Agricultural Extension Services and all the other teachers and trainers who act in a similar capacity. It gathers together the background knowledge necessary for a basic understanding of what pests and diseases are, the agents which cause them and the principles of combatting them. Then it demonstrates practical methods of pest and disease control in detail. Finally it gives examples and solutions of the problems in a village context. These can be used by extension staff in their own work.

In choosing which materials to introduce the guide has been availability. Products which are hard to find are not advocated – the exception being the knapsack sprayer, for which no useful alternative exists. References and suggestions for further reading are listed in the bibliography.

To the Instructor
About the cartoons

At the end of each unit you will find the examples referred to, in the form of an illustrated story presented as a strip cartoon or 'comic-strip'. Comic strip has been a tool in the hands of educators for many years, but only in 1980 was a lengthy study published that examined the qualities, 'sophistication, flexibility, fantasy and dynamic style', to quote the authors, that make it so effective in communication.

If you are a qualified agricultural instructor the strip cartoons are not there to convey new technical information to you, they are there to show and hand out to your **farmers, trainees** or **students**. Let them see the pages and take them through the stories. If you use drama or storytelling as an extension or teaching method, the strip cartoon could be the starting point for your own expanded play, story or educational comic strip.

We give permission to photocopy or trace **the strip cartoon pages**, but only these pages, to use in a class, demonstration, discussion, for private study or to hand out to your farmers. To distinguish these pages clearly they have a grey tint on the edge and the words '© Robin Edwards and Rosalyn Rappaport 1992' at the bottom. You must make sure that these words also appear on any copy you make.

About the record sheets

These serve as models; your own situation will be in many respects unique and you will need to vary the contents or format. If you are an extension agent, first discuss the sheet carefully with the cooperating grower. Explain why the information is needed and which items are most important. When you collect the completed sheet look it over and discuss with the farmer any items that strike you as interesting. To the best of your ability answer questions. There is a saying 'knowledge is power'. You have the power to take rural development a stage further.

Introducing the characters in the strip cartoons. For an explanation of the cartoons see 'How to use this book' on the previous page.

Here are **Ali**, his wife **Leila** and their daughter **Miri**.

And here are their neighbours, **Peter**, **Sarah** and their children **Joseph**, **Amalia** and baby. Joseph and Miri were married last year.

I am **Suzie** the farmer's insect eating friend who gets rid of flies and grubs for him. I am not at all like those birds that guzzle his seeds.

Our visiting foreigner, **Ingrid**, works at the clinic. Her father is a farmer – like us. She says that's why she likes it here.

This is **John** the extension agent from the Ministry of Agriculture. He visits us and occasionally gets a good idea from somewhere; from farmers, from his books or from his work, who knows?

Acknowledgements

Among those who helped me generously with facts, advice and time I remember gratefully George Grimmet of the British Council, Dr Jim Hoxeng of USAID, Professor Weltzien of Bonn University, Dr Philip Harris of the Henry Doubleday Research Association, Dr Lucy Ambridge of the Natural Resource Institute, the director, engineers and salesmen of Cooper Pegler Ltd, and Dr Chris Garforth at Reading University.

Picture Acknowledgements

Natural Crop Protection in the Tropics, Stroll, G. 1988 Margraf. Fig 9.3(a)

Flora of West Tropical Africa, Hutchinson, J. and Dalziel, J. M. 1927 Crown Agents. Fig. 9.2

Reafforestation in Arid Lands, Weber, F. R. and Storey, C. Fig. 9.3b

African Gardens and Orchards, Duprez, H. and de Leener, 1989, Macmillan. Fig. 12.4

Agroforestry and Dryland Africa, Rocheleau, D. et al. 1988. ICRAF. Fig. 19.1

Hydraulic Sprayers, British Crop Protection Council 1985. Figs. 7.2, 7.3, 7.4, 7.6, 7.7, 7.8.

Cooper Pegler Ltd, Burgess Hill, Sussex, U.K. Figs. 7.6, 7.7 and 7.8.

PESTS

UNIT 1 Introduction to insects and spiders

It is hard to believe that a caterpillar and a moth should be the same creature but it is so. The moth is the adult and the caterpillar (or larva) is the juvenile form.

THE TOMATO FRUIT WORM

In the adult stage insect bodies are divided into three parts and they have six legs. Most have wings (Fig. 1.1a). They are related to spiders which have eight legs (Fig. 1.1b).

Nearly all adult insects live in the air or on land but many of their young live in fresh water. The females of most insects lay eggs, after mating, which hatch into worm-like larvae called grubs or caterpillars (Fig. 1.2). This is sexual reproduction. Some insects, after mating, bear offspring that resemble the adult but have undeveloped wings. These young insects are known as nymphs. A few insects lay fertile eggs or bear nymphs without mating. This manner of multiplying is asexual reproduction or parthenogenesis. Aphids reproduce in this way.

When larvae are ready to develop into adults they enter an apparently 'resting' phase inside a protective case called the pupa or chrysalis. Inside the pupal case a larva develops into an adult and when fully developed, splits open the case and emerges. This may take days, weeks or months depending on the insect and the climate.

Insects show great variety in their life cycles and in what they eat and where they live. They are very adaptable to different conditions. Many chew plants and those that chew crops are pests (harmful to man). Some insects, such as the honey bee and those whose larvae eat weeds or the larvae of pests are beneficial (useful to man). When insects feed on the nectar in flowers they help to pollinate the flower and produce seeds, so a moth or butterfly may be beneficial even though its larvae are harmful.

Insects which eat plants can be divided into various classes.

- Caterpillars and leaf miners, that eat plant parts above ground.
- Fruit worms and stem borers, which burrow into the plant.
- Cutworms and termites, which chew plants below or at ground level.
- Aphids and scale insects, that suck plant juices.
- Disease carriers. Just as mosquitoes carry the malaria parasite from one person to another so insects, particularly aphids, carry virus diseases from one plant to another.

Insects can become serious pests because they may lay thousands of eggs in a short space of time. They grow rapidly, producing a large number of offspring which need a lot of food as fuel for this process. They can spread far by the winged adult stages. Their great variety and adaptability enables them to take advantage of new conditions very quickly. Farmers who grow crops in monoculture (cover large areas with the same plant) provide ideal feeding and breeding opportunities for insects already adapted to other members of the same plant family.

Spiders are mainly carnivorous and eat insects; but the spider family includes the mites, which suck plant juices. These are, therefore, also pests. Spider mites share many characteristics with insect pests and can be treated as such when growers must fight an infestation.

Creatures, such as birds and spiders that eat insects are the grower's allies. There are also insects which eat other insects these are carnivorous. None of these should be killed unnecessarily. It is often impossible to avoid them when spraying but careful use of cultural pest controls (Unit 5), careful choice of spray chemicals (Units 8 to 11), and the use of correct spraying methods (Unit 7), will keep damage to these helpful creatures low and reduce the need to spray.

The weather also affects pests. Their food plants may be wiped out by flood or fire. Air temperature may be too high or too low for survival. The soil where they lay their eggs may dry out. Practises such as weeding, interplanting, ridging, mulching, spacing and choice of planting date all modify the micro-climate (Fig. 15.1), and help to keep pest numbers down.

The best method or combination of methods to control a pest depends on its life cycle. There are times at which the pest will be vulnerable (easy to kill) to sprays and other times at which it is protected from sprays but not from mechanical damage. The pests illustrated in Units 1–5 were chosen because they are widespread, serious pests and their life cycles are typical of insects that damage crops.

There is a saying that 'prevention is better than cure.' Knowing the life cycle of a target pest (one the grower wishes to kill), makes it clear how cultural methods prevent pest outbreaks, and how chemical methods (sprays, dusts and baits) cure an outbreak. All control methods must be chosen with regard to the insect and its habits. Efforts to find a universal and simple cure for insect attack are illusiory.

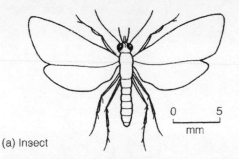

(a) Insect

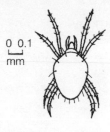

(b) Mite

(a) Insect bodies are divided into head, thorax and abdomen. The six legs are attached to the thorax. Most have wings though not all can fly.

(b) Mites are tiny spiders. Most spiders are carnivorous but mites are an exception. They live by sucking plant sap. They have 8 legs and spin fine threads which help them to float on air to feeding sites.

Fig. 1.1   Differences between insects and spiders

A

B

C

D

E

F

A The moths mate.
B The eggs are laid singly or in small clusters on the leaves.
C The eggs hatch in about 4 days and the larvae disperse seeking the fruits. On the way some leaves are chewed.

D On reaching a fruit the larvae pierce the skin and burrow into the fruit. They are now safe from spray and predators.
E On reaching full growth the larvae leave the fruits and crawl to the ground where they pupate under leaf litter.

F When the change from larva to adult has taken place the pupal case splits and the adult moth emerges. It flies off to feed and to find a mate.

Fig. 1.2   The life cycle of the tomato fruit worm (*Heliothis araigera*)

4

The tomato fruit worm (Fig. 1.2) is a serious pest with a life cycle typical of fruit borers. Its larvae eat into beans, cotton and okra as well as tomatoes. The adult is a moth. In arid lands its season is restricted and predictable but in wet climates it can breed new generations continually. In small gardens the caterpillars can be controlled by daily inspections, by 'rubbing out' egg clusters and young larvae and removing pierced fruits from the field. In large gardens the practical solution is to spray early, the moment the larvae or any damage to fruit is noticed. Pierced fruits must always be removed from the garden. It is wise to look through the field several times a week during the danger season and monitor (make a rough count of) the pests or any damage they may have done.

Details of sprays and safety precautions are given in Units 7, 8 and 10. Before spraying take note of the rules for safe spraying detailed in Unit 7.

UNIT 2   Mechanical controls

Spraying is not always the best way to cure a pest attack. An insect that is large enough to be seen easily, or that lays its eggs in clusters, or whose larvae congregate, can be eradicated mechanically. At a convenient stage of its life cycle it can be picked from the leaves and crushed.

This method works admirably with *Papilio demodocus* the orange dog (Fig. 2.1). It can be used even on mature trees in orchards of several hectares.

In Zambia for instance, four workers kept three hectares of citrus clean with a weekly 'pick-over' during the pests's season. Although the pickers could reach only the lower branches it was evident that natural predators were clearing the larvae from the higher branches. The harvest was good and the fruit unblemished though trees only half a kilometre from the plantation were being totally stripped of leaves and never yielded fruit.

Hand collection is cheap and precise it is light work. The disadvantage is that it uses a lot of labour, but for the family farmer this is often not a problem. Other mechanical methods include:

'Rubbing out' egg clusters. Many insect eggs are light coloured and easy to see if laid in clusters. Some species lay their eggs on the upper and some on the lower sides of leaves so inspection must be done with care. After hatching the larvae remain grouped for a while before dispersing. With luck they can be 'rubbed out' at this stage too.

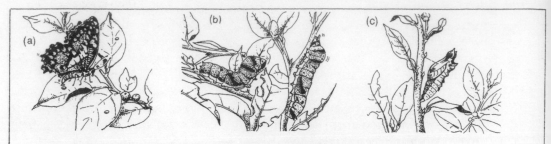

The adult *Papilio demodocus* (a), is a handsome brown butterfly with yellow marks, often seen feeding on various flowers. Its eggs are white and 1 mm in diameter. They are laid singly on the upper side of new flush leaves of citrus and hatch in four days.

The caterpillar (b), is pale green with black patches. It grows, in 30 days, to its full length of 5 cm. The pupa (c), is yellow-green or brown and 3 cm long. It fixes itself by a thread to a twig or branch for some 14 days before the adult emerges.

Fig. 2.1   The orange dog caterpillar

The exclusion of air   from grain-storage pots. This is done by packing grain, together with dust or fine sand, in clay pots which are then sealed. Once the pot is full of grain fine dust is poured into it and shaken down so that the gaps between the grain are filled. If insects hatch they suffocate. This treatment is also described in Unit 11.

Dusting with abrasive powder   Finely ground laterite earth works well. It rubs the waxy outer layer from insect bodies and they dehydrate (lose moisture) and die. It has been observed in village grain stores that insects will not bore into grains dusted in this manner nor lay eggs on them. To coat grain thoroughly before storage shake 10 k of grain in a sack together with 1 k of fine laterite dust. Pounded ashes work equally well.

Grease bands   placed round the trunks of fruit trees protect them from ants or caterpillars that attempt to reach the leaves by crawling up the trunks.

Ditching   Army worms and cut-worms (Fig. 5.2), that migrate into crops by crawling along the ground, can be trapped in ditches dug round the plants. Once trapped they can be crushed or sprayed. Seedlings are protected in this way because the area to be protected is small. The side of the ditch nearest the crop must be straight, though it need not be more than 10 cm deep. The worms cannot crawl up a sheer slope.

Light hoeing   will disclose pests. The egg cases of grasshoppers which are 2 to 3 cm long can be found in this way round cassava plants. They can then be removed or left to dry in the sun.

7

UNIT 3   Sap suckers

Some insects and spiders harm plants by sucking sap and taking up food that the plant has made by photosynthesis. This action starves the plant and can inject toxins and provide entry points for disease organisms.

The damage to crops is not as easily seen as is the leaf stripping done by caterpillars, but the slow starvation can result in stunted, unproductive plants.

Sap suckers extract the sap in different ways:

- Aphids (Fig. 3.1) pierce the delicate, unprotected surfaces of tender buds and young shoots, and suck sap directly from the cells.
- Thrips (Fig. 3.2) rasp away leaf surfaces and drink the sap that runs from the wounds.
- Spider mites (Fig. 1.1b) feed by sucking the sap from leaves or, in some cases, flowers.
- Scale insects, such as mealy bugs, common pests of citrus, coffee and pineapple, suck sap while protected by their waxy or scaly coats.
- Whiteflies, attack cassava in the same way covering the stems with white scales.

Aphids   are soft bodied insects 1–2 cm long, coloured green, brown or black according to type. Some are winged but many have no wings. They reproduce asexually and their offspring also reproduce asexually; thus very large numbers are rapidly produced. The nymphs are 1–2 cm long. They collect where they were born on new growth and feed without moving; often entirely coating the young growth with their bodies (Fig 3.1). Buds are distorted and never grow well. The sugars made by photosynthesis (Unit 4) never reach their destinations at the growing points; the whole plant is starved and weakened. In addition, aphids can inject diseases (Unit 13) which can do more damage than the feeding, for while that may reduce the crop, viruses can destroy it.

As they feed aphids excrete sugary wastes on which fungi flourish. These parasitic plants coat the leaves with the unsightly black powder of their spores and in this way prevent photosynthesis. Aphids are washed off by heavy rain showers and, being soft bodied, dry up easily. They are found on the underside of leaves where they are protected from wind and sun.

A few aphids will not affect yields and can be ignored, but if a pest-sized population seems to be building up the crop should be sprayed with soapy water or, if necessary, insecticide.

Winged females produce wingless juveniles (nymphs), that feed without moving from the feeding site.

In their turn the nymphs produce more nymphs. In 5 days one aphid can become over 100 aphids.

They feed on the tender, actively growing shoots and leaves, congregating in shade and on the underside of leaves.

When numbers outrun food supply winged forms reappear and migrate to nearby plants to renew the growth cycle.

Fig. 3.1   Aphids. The life cycle – asexual reproduction

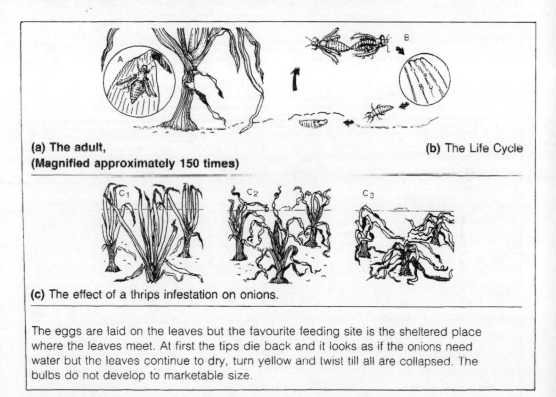

(a) The adult,
(Magnified approximately 150 times)

(b) The Life Cycle

(c) The effect of a thrips infestation on onions.

The eggs are laid on the leaves but the favourite feeding site is the sheltered place where the leaves meet. At first the tips die back and it looks as if the onions need water but the leaves continue to dry, turn yellow and twist till all are collapsed. The bulbs do not develop to marketable size.

Fig. 3.2   Thrips

Thrips are brown and about 1 mm long, with thin fringed wings. They mate and lay their eggs on stems or leaves, preferring, in onions, the point where the leaf wraps round other leaves. They will feed on tobacco, tomato, cotton and other plants but are a serious pest only on onions. The nymphs are white or yellow and can produce a new generation every three weeks, if weather conditions are suitable. The signs of their presence are silvery flecks on the leaves where the surface has been rasped away. As the pests increase the leaves dry, twist, distort and wilt from the tip down (Fig. 3.2c). Infested onions do not develop good bulbs.

Spider mites are only just visible without a magnifying glass. The eggs are laid singly and stuck to the underside of leaves with a strand of web. The adult lives for about three weeks and can lay 200 eggs. They feed all together on the underside of leaves. Cotton, cassava, date palms, coffee and tea can all suffer from this pest. Yellow patches appear and spread until the leaves turn red and fall.

UNIT 4   Insect injury to photosynthesis

There is a proverb that says, 'all flesh is grass' because all food eaten by animals can be traced back to green plants. Only green plants (and a few bacteria and algae), can make food out of the basic elements by using the energy from sunlight to change carbon dioxide – a gas forming part of air – plus water into sugars. The process is called photosynthesis, and is carried out in the leaves and other green parts of the plant.

With the addition of very small quantities of minerals from the soil (nitrogen in the form of nitrates is particularly important), sugars and proteins are created and used by the plant to build the materials of which it is made: cellulose in cell walls, lignin in wood, starch in tubers, oils in seeds, growth regulating enzymes, waxes which waterproof the leaves, and so on.

Once made, the sugars and other products of photosynthesis disperse into the sap which carries them through stems, branches and trunks to wherever they are needed to help form flowers, fruit, seeds, new shoots, colours, sweet or sharp tastes, and so on.

A tree has many more leaves than it needs and can lose some without harm to itself, but there is a limit. If too many leaves are destroyed then the tree stops growing and never develops flowers and fruit. Weak trees and small plants may die. Fig. 4.1 shows a situation very common in small

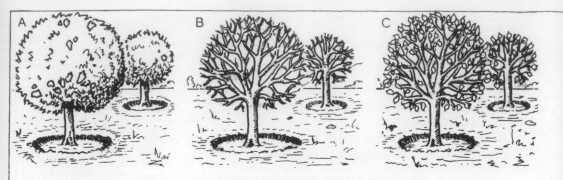

Young citrus trees (a), defoliated by the caterpillar (b), put out leaves in the next growing season (c), and these, in their turn, are eaten and the trees defoliated.

2nd year   3rd year   4th year

Year after year the trees struggle against the loss of all or most of their leaves. They do not die but they do not grow or develop flowers or fruit. In less serious infestations the trees grow, but very slowly – and give very little fruit.

Fig. 4.1 Defoliation of citrus by the orange dog caterpillar (*Papilio demodocus*)

citrus orchards. The trees grow well till the caterpillars discover them – often at the time of transplanting – after that they never thrive. Year after year the new growth of leaves is eaten and the tree remains nearly the same size as it was when first planted. This situation continues unless the caterpillar – in this case the orange dog – is controlled. Then the trees resume growth and start fruiting.

Caterpillars (Units 1 and 2) destroy the photosynthetic process by eating the leaf or by grazing its surface. Their numbers must be kept below the point at which so many leaves are destroyed that plant growth is slowed

Inspect the trees. As soon as the first caterpillar is seen go through the orchard weekly, knocking them from the leaves and crushing them underfoot.

The remainder, those that were overlooked or were out of reach on higher branches, will be eaten by natural predators.

or halted, but they need not be eradicated. Slight browsing may be beneficial because healthy plants respond by developing new shoots and leaves. The power of plants to recuperate was seen in an extreme case in Ethiopia when ground-nuts razed by locusts, put out new shoots and gave a higher than normal yield.

Sucking insects and stem borers affect growth and development processes other than photosynthesis.

UNIT 5 Integrated pest management

Integrated pest management (IPM) is designed:

To prevent insect numbers from increasing to levels where they destroy the quality or yield of crops.

To develop protection methods that use the existing natural controls.

To combine cultural practises with carefully chosen sprays in a way that supports existing natural controls.

By the end of a normal growing season, there would be vast numbers of herbivorous (plant eating) insects were it not that they are hunted by birds, carnivorous insects and spiders, and are killed by heat, cold, wind, dust, floods, rains, fire and disease microorganisms. They are also checked by poisons in plants that prevent them from feeding, breeding or completing their life cycles.

Everything growers do to their crops influences the insect populations in their fields; the chances of a good harvest improve when nature is made an ally in the protection process. Knowing how natural forces affect insect survival is the start of pest control.

IPM does not aim to eradicate pests, but to keep them below economic level – the level at which crop losses are noticeable. The word 'management' is chosen to describe this kind of control.

The guiding rules of Integrated Pest Management are:
1. Only the pest should be killed by the control methods used.
2. No part of the environment, plant or animal, should suffer undue damage from the control methods used.
3. Cultural controls, which prevent infestations are preferred to chemical controls, which cure infestations. Spraying and dusting are the last resort of crop protection, not the only means.
4. Plantings of well adapted native varieties should be undertaken to compensate the environment for plants cleared to make room for crops.

Thinking on IPM grew out of the alarming experiences of the years between 1940, when DDT was discovered, and the 1960's, when it became clear that it was a threat to health. (See *Silent Spring* by R. Carson in the Bibliography.) The facts influenced the public and the agricultural community and caused changes in the laws regulating man-made pesticides.

We have discovered through research that natural forces limit insect populations more effectively than do spray programmes. Under natural circumstances often less than 5% of insect eggs survive to become adults.

Natural factors that limit insect numbers

1. Birds consume vast quantities of flies, larvae and pupae. On the ground ducks and chickens, in the air swifts and parrots, hunt and eat insects.

2. Carnivorous insects eat insects, just as carnivorous animals eat their prey.

3. Parasitic insects lay their eggs in the bodies of insects. When the larvae hatch they eat the paralysed host insects. Disease organisms too, attack insects.

4. Some plants are poisonous to insects (Unit 8).

5. Insect diet is often limited to the plants of one family or one variety. The banana weevil, *Cosmopolidus sordidus*, as far as is known, can live only on bananas; the citrus psyllid, *Trioza erytreae*, eats only members of the Rutaceae, the citrus family.

6. Healthy plants resist disease and recover from insect attacks; unhealthy plants do neither.

7. Genetic resistance is found permanently in the plant and passed on in the seed. This develops in some plants.

8. Temperature and humidity restrict insect breeding. Small changes in either can cause the disappearance of a pest from a district.

9. Fire, flood, frost and other climatic conditions destroy eggs and pupae.
   These facts dictate our choice of pest management. The following section describes how growers exploit these facts to their advantage.

Cultural practises that control pests

Planting and seeding

1. Selecting healthy seed results in healthy plants, which are more resistant to attacks whether of insects, diseases or climate, than weak plants. For instance, plants growing vigorously respond to insect grazing by putting out new and more numerous shoots.

2. Selecting healthy cuttings (Unit 15) gives similar protection. Cuttings from plants seen to be clear of surrounding insect infestation may have genetic resistance.

3. Storing seed cleanly ensures that it is not weakened by boring insects nor infected by bacteria and viruses (Unit 13). Infected seedlings will have a poor start. Many will die. Those that grow will yield poorly and the pest will increase as the crop declines. Good storage practises include:

• Dusting with chemicals, whether commercial or made on the farm from plant or mineral materials.

- Dusting with abrasives.
- Sealing in air-tight containers.
- Coating with vegetable oils (Unit 8).

4. Care in transplanting Uprooted plants recover swiftly if they are kept moist and replanted without delay (Fig. 15.2). Rooting materials, pineapple shoots for example, could be dipped in chemical before replanting so that soil-born pests will not be transferred to the new site.

5. Planting dates can sometimes be chosen so that insects known to be pests of that particular crop are not in season at the crucial time.

Maintenance and cultivation

1. Weeding within crops disturbs insect breeding and pupation and lets in light, warmth and air currents. This discourages insects (and diseases), that prefer cool, wet, shady conditions. Clearing a margin round the crop disturbs the breeding of cutworms which could migrate from the bush into the crop. It deprives insects (and fungi), of plants that could serve as alternate hosts – wild members of the crop's plant family for instance or naturally seeded plants from previous crops. These help pests to survive between seasons.

2. Cultivation with the hoe stirs the top layers of soil and disturbs grubs or pupae on the surface or ones lightly buried. They dry up or are exposed to predators (Fig. 5.2).

3. Ploughing turns the soil and exposes grubs and pupae at deeper levels. Birds follow the plough picking off weed seeds as well as grubs and pupae.

4. Crop hygiene A field must be clean when the crop goes in and must stay clean during the life of the crop. Damaged and fallen plant parts cannot be allowed to lie because they provide shelter at the soil surface as also do fruits already pierced or stems already bored. Thorough clearing is practical after the crop has been lifted. Hot-composting residues (Fig. 14.1), or burning, or removing them to animal pens, ensures that insects, eggs or pupae do not survive to infect the next crop. The same rule applies to bush clearance.

5. Livestock are an essential part of farm operations. Whether pastured on harvest residues or allowed to forage, cattle and poultry add manure and reduce the insect population by eating a good part of it. In China ducks are driven through the young rice to grub up insects.

6. Rotation Most insects prefer one type or family of plant over others. So planting different crops in succession on the same land breaks pest reproduction cycles. Crops chosen to go into a rotation must not be so closely related that they attract the same pests. Since eggs and pupae can survive in the soil across seasons it is wise to make a rotation last over at least four crops.

7. Intercropping or barrier planting, is widely practised throughout the tropics and is increasingly recommended as a control method in temperate agriculture. Growing two crops side by side creates obstacles for pests that can slow or even halt their progress across a field. This can be because the barrier plant is too high or is chemically distasteful (for example, cabbage moths avoid the scent of tomato plants), or because host plants are harder to find. Even aphids, that attack almost any crop, are slowed down by interplanting. Interplanting schemes are many and depend on crop, climate, and economic judgment.

8. Resistant varieties Within any plant population some plants resist pests (and diseases) more than others. Growers have selected and bred from these plants and sell the seeds as special varieties. If a field is heavily infected, yet some plants seem to have escaped damage, it could be wise to collect seeds or cuttings and grow them separately for a few seasons to see if they are indeed resistant to attack.

9. Ridging drains the soil immediately round the roots. It creates a microclimate unfavourable to organisms needing moist conditions.

10. Manuring with dung or with crops grown specially for the purpose and ploughed in (green manuring) adds fertility to the soil and helps to produce healthy, disease resistant plants.

All these practices lessen a pest's chance to establish itself in overwhelming numbers; they are preventative. If however, in spite of such measures an insect becomes a pest, spraying and dusting, essentially curative practises, must be undertaken.

Chemical controls in integrated pest management

Spraying insecticides demands skill and knowledge if money is to be spent wisely and problems avoided. It is necessary to know how the chemicals behave and what they can do and when and how to apply them. Units 8 to 11 cover the first two points and Unit 7 describes the safe and proper way to apply the chemicals.

Increasingly it is found that after an area has been repeatedly sprayed against a particular pest with the same chemical one or more of the following situations arise:

1. The pest population drops, but then recovers and increases.
2. The pest is not killed as easily as at first; more frequent spraying of stronger mixtures is needed to get good results. The insect is said to have developed resistance to the chemical.
3. The pest is eradicated, but another insect takes its place.
4. Bird populations decline so allowing plant and cattle pests to increase. Honey bee numbers fall.

The reason for these unhappy results, which can destroy crops or, at the least, increase the expense and work burden of growers, is to be found in a study of food chains. This is shown in Fig 5.1.

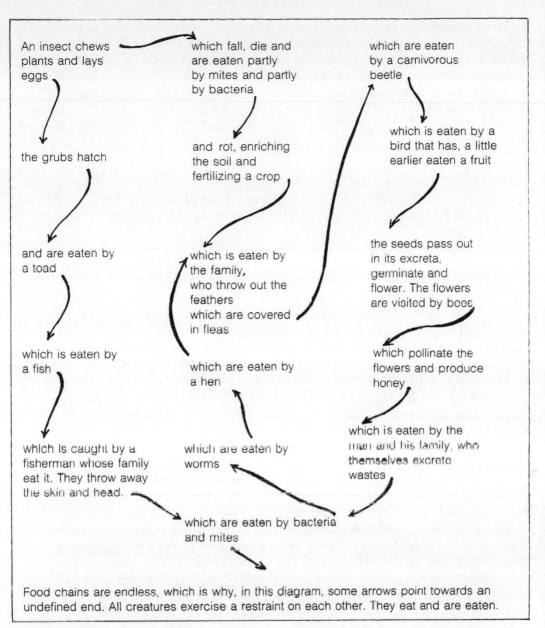

An insect chews plants and lays eggs

which fall, die and are eaten partly by mites and partly by bacteria

which are eaten by a carnivorous beetle

the grubs hatch

and rot, enriching the soil and fertilizing a crop

which is eaten by a bird that has, a little earlier eaten a fruit

and are eaten by a toad

which is eaten by the family, who throw out the feathers which are covered in fleas

the seeds pass out in its excreta, germinate and flower. The flowers are visited by bees

which is eaten by a fish

which are eaten by a hen

which pollinate the flowers and produce honey

which is caught by a fisherman whose family eat it. They throw away the skin and head.

which are eaten by worms

which is eaten by the man and his family, who themselves excrete wastes

which are eaten by bacteria and mites

Food chains are endless, which is why, in this diagram, some arrows point towards an undefined end. All creatures exercise a restraint on each other. They eat and are eaten.

Fig. 5.1 Food chains

On those occasions when only the application of insecticides can save a crop, careful growers will heed the following:

- Avoid, as far as possible, insecticides known as broad spectrum, that kill birds, spiders and mammals as well as insects. They can kill livestock and seriously disrupt food chains. They may be dangerous to children.
- Avoid persistent compounds – chemicals that take a long time to break down. While they remain on a plant all insects which come in contact with them will die including any beneficial ones.

- Because very often there is no choice but to use broad spectrum insecticides, growers must spray so that only the crop at risk is covered. Bush and forest areas, as well as fields outside the crop boundaries, should be untouched. Wind can carry the spray droplets a long way. Details of how to spray with maximum safety to the user and the surroundings are given in Unit 7.

The cutworm provides a good example of a pest against which a purely chemical attack is of very limited use and which can be controlled only by combining cultural and chemical protection methods. Fig 5.2 illustrates this integration of methods.

Pest control, the environment and management decisions

Farmers are land managers and must always consider the long term effects of their management. Land that is not used with thought for its natural regional adaptation will be degraded, that is to say, will become less easy to live in and to farm. Everything on earth has its niche (place in the system), and all living things are interrelated.

Farmers, by the nature of their employment, change the environment so they must work with an eye to the future, not only of the farm but of the region. Only if they take correct management decisions will the improvements they make be permanent. The key is knowledge, therefore farmers must appreciate the following facts:

- The farm cannot be separated from its region. The crops a farmer chooses and the way they are cultivated have effects beyond farm boundaries. For example, growers who plant cabbages increase the population of cabbage eating insects for the whole district.
- Concentration on large-scale production of one crop year after year can, within a lifetime, increase pest problems to the point where cultivation becomes impossible and villages are depopulated as the next generation leaves to seek work elsewhere. This type of farm management, known as monoculture, rules out the use of techniques such as rotation and intercropping. Farmers are obliged to spray and buy chemical fertilizers in ever increasing amounts simply to keep yields at levels that will give enough to live on. Inputs (the things one buys or the work one does in order to obtain a harvest) then cost so much that the promise of high income is never fulfilled. Pest problems spiral out of control.
- Farming in accord with the environment can mean planting crops in suitable sites rather than adapting sites to desired crops. Growing locally developed crop varieties rather than exotic hybrids, controlling pests by intercropping (an imitation of natural plant arrangement) will reduce pest population. Soil fertility will be maintained by fallowing, by ploughing in residues and dung, and by pasturing animals on harvested land rather than by spreading chemical fertilizers. All these practises help to grow good crops in the future.

20

 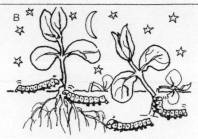

(a) Eggs are laid under trash or on the underside of leaves from where the caterpillars descend and burrow into the soil.

(b) During the day they stay underground and at night come to the surface to feed on young stems. Older grubs eat roots.

(c) On reaching their full size – about 4 cm, they go underground or under trash to pupate.

(d) Eight days later the moth emerges to mate and lay eggs. She can lay up to 1000 eggs.

(e) A month before planting, dig or plough to a depth of at least 10 cm. When the earth is turned the grubs are revealed to predators.

(f) Clear nearby bush to dislodge grubs or pupae. This also deprives the females of egg laying sites.

(g) Spray young plants to kill any eggs or grubs that might have reached the nursery bed.

(h) Round small areas, such as nursery beds, lay a barrier of poison bait.

Fig. 5.2 The life cycle of the cutworm and Integrated Controls to avoid infestation

22

- Traditional farming systems round the world contain within themselves the seeds of their own improved practices. Building on established local knowledge is the basis of good development.
- Know all aspects of a pest's life cycle. For example, it is a waste of time and money to spray against fruit fly if infected fruits are left in the field. Similarly, if a pest feeds on the underside of leaves it is useless to spray only from above.
- Monitor the crop regularly and use judgement as to whether a pest, even if it has done some damage, needs controling or whether it can be tolerated. Control measures should always relate to the value of the crop.

Summary of units 1 to 5   Insect pests and Integrated Pest Management

1. Insects have six legs, most have wings and they have life cycles that include a resting stage. They can reproduce themselves sexually, or asexually, but in either way reproduce at a very high rate. Some eat other insects, but most feed on plants.
2. Spiders are similar to insects, but are mainly carnivorous. They have eight legs and spin silk webs or threads. Some very tiny spiders, called mites, are herbivorous.
3. Loss of leaves, through insect feeding, deprives plants of the power to photosynthesise, while loss of sap destroys sugars. Either way growth is halted.
4. Insect populations are limited by natural enemies such as birds and spiders and weather. In crops, husbandry – all agricultural activities from land preparation to harvest – also controls insect numbers.
5. The long-term, indescriminate use of broad-spectrum insecticides creates pest populations which are no longer killed by that chemical. Because their natural enemies may also have been killed the pest populations can be larger than before.
6. Sprays can be specific in action, that is, kill the pest and leave all other insects, including the natural enemies of the pest, untouched.
7. The combination of husbandry with controlled spraying forms a system of crop protection known as Integrated Pest Management (IPM).
8. Integrated Pest Management gives crops long lasting protection without damaging after-effects. It saves the farmer money and preserves or improves his environment.
9. Informed judgement is critically important when deciding which farming system to employ and if and when to spray.
10. There are occasions when farmers decide in favour of capital intensive systems. It is not the purpose of this section to say that they should not do this, but only that if they do, they will inevitably have to meet the expenses of land rehabilitation if their property is to retain its worth to themselves and their children.

SPRAY EQUIPMENT

UNIT 6 Handmade spray tools

This unit describes two handmade sprayers that can be made on the farm, for little or no money. In one method water is flicked over the crops with a bunch of fine twigs (Fig. 6.1). In the other the water is sprayed from a plastic bottle whose lid has been pierced with five or six needle holes (Fig. 6.2).

Hand-made spray tools provide growers who do not have factory made sprayers with the means to apply pesticides. Compared with commercial sprayers they make the work slow and they are more suited to be used with a few plants than in a large vegetable garden. They are for use only with soap and water insecticide, or sodium bicarbonate fungicide solution. With any other mixture, whether commercial or made on the farm, their use is dangerous.

Advantages are low cost and availability, but they have some disadvantages:

- Rather than spray cones they produce jets, which in the case of the plastic bottle, must be broken into sprinkles by a shake of the hand. These sprinkles are composed of very big droplets. Because smaller droplets cover a plant more efficiently than do larger ones, it is not easy to cover a plant really well by this method.
- The water is squeezed or shaken out with only a hand's strength and so cannot go far.
- The spray comes in bursts, rather than in a stream, so that the user must stand, rather than walk among the plants, while spraying.
- The spray does not easily reach the underside of the leaves.
- It is impossible to avoid wetting hands and clothes while flicking water over plants and holding back leaves in order to spray the underside. For this reason handmade spray tools must be used only with soap and water or soap-water-disinfectant insecticides (Units 9–10), or sodium bicarbonate fungicide (Unit 14).

The plastic bottle has some advantages over twig bunches.

- It is easier to control and direct the spray from a plastic bottle.
- It is easier to spray upwards onto the underside of the leaves.
- The work is quicker.

- The user may make bottles that produce different spray patterns; some with one hole, giving a single jet, others with more holes, giving sprays. Different designs may suit different purposes.
- A plastic bottle may be used as a 'puffer' device to spread powders.

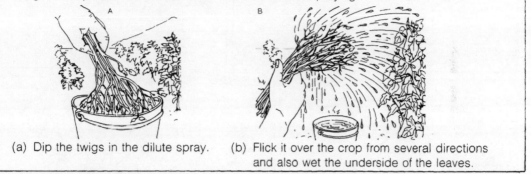

Use this method only with soap and water or very dilute disinfectant insecticides or with sodium bicarbonate. Even though these mixtures do not harm the skin or present any danger from poison users must wash their hands after spraying.

A

B

(a) Dip the twigs in the dilute spray.

(b) Flick it over the crop from several directions and also wet the underside of the leaves.

Fig. 6.1 Using a bunch of twigs to scatter pesticides

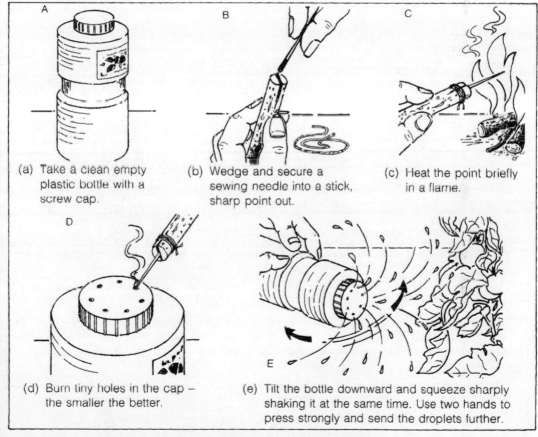

(a) Take a clean empty plastic bottle with a screw cap.

(b) Wedge and secure a sewing needle into a stick, sharp point out.

(c) Heat the point briefly in a flame.

(d) Burn tiny holes in the cap – the smaller the better.

(e) Tilt the bottle downward and squeeze sharply shaking it at the same time. Use two hands to press strongly and send the droplets further.

Fig. 6.2 Making a hand sprayer from a plastic bottle

© Robin Edmonds, Rosalyn Rappaport 1992

26

UNIT 7 Hydraulic knapsack sprayers

In hydraulic sprayers liquid is forced through fine holes in a nozzle and comes out as a cloud of tiny droplets. In hydraulic knapsack sprayers the pressure is created by the user working a lever up and down.

Knapsack sprayers can be worked either by piston or diaphragm pumps. Pistons are less practical than diaphragms, but there are on the market a lot of knapsack sprayers that depend on piston pumps, so before the grower makes a choice or lays down money he should know which type he is getting.

A piston pump   can create high pressures and a mist of very fine droplets. This can be a disadvantage as the droplets hang in the air and the operator runs the risk of breathing in the spray. A mist drifts on the lightest breeze and this makes it hard to control and confine to the plants being sprayed. Finally, pistons are vulnerable to grit and abrasion and their parts are difficult to repair and expensive to replace.

A diaphragm pump   (Fig 7.1) creates medium pressures and larger droplets. Users can keep clear of the spray cloud because it goes where directed and settles fairly quickly. On most models two pressures are available – medium and low. An adjustment device above the relief valve (Fig. 7.3) controls this change. (The lower pressure is used for applying herbicides.)

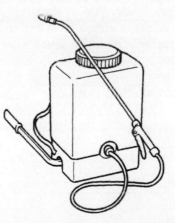

Fig. 7.1   A diaphragm sprayer

The diaphragm has no sliding surfaces as does the piston and cylinder. It therefore has fewer surfaces that could be worn away by trapped grit or dirt.

Droplet size is important because the smaller the droplet the more efficiently the crop is covered with spray and so the greater is the protection. Droplets can, however, be so small that they remain in the air for a long time, endangering the spray operator and anyone working nearby. Droplet size is governed by pressure – higher pressures producing smaller droplets – but also by the type of nozzle used. The nozzles commonly supplied with manually operated diaphragm pump sprayers form cones of larger droplets. Operators should still cover their noses when spraying.

The diaphragm and its associated parts are easy to reach, disassemble and replace.

How the diaphragm sprayer works (Fig. 7.2)

The lever's upstroke draws the flexible diaphragm down, which enlarges the space between the diaphragm and the pressure valve, and so lowers pressure in this space. The suction valve opens and admits water from the tank into this space – which is in fact the pressure cylinder. The pressure cylinder is shown in some detail in Fig. 7.6.

The lever's downstroke pushes the diaphragm up, which decreases the space between the diaphragm and the pressure valve and so increases the pressure there. The suction valve is pushed closed, and the pressure valve pushed open. Liquid is sucked out of the pressure cylinder and into the pressure chamber. The air trapped in the pressure chamber is squashed or compressed a little.

Further strokes of the lever force liquid into the pressure chamber. This compresses the air trapped inside. Air is elastic and acts like a spring; the harder it is compressed the more strongly it expands if released. When the air will not compress much further the lever becomes difficult to work. The experienced user soon learns by the feel on the lever, when that point has been reached and the trigger can be worked to release pressure and produce a good spray. The built up pressure can be released in two ways, either.

- the relief valve (Figs 7.2, 7.3) opens, allowing water to flow back into the tank, or
- the user presses the trigger and releases spray onto the crop (Fig. 7.2).

It is air pressure, not the direct action of the lever, that forces out the spray, and it is the 'cushioning' effect of the compressed air that pushes the spray out through the nozzle in a steady stream.

1. The tank is filled.

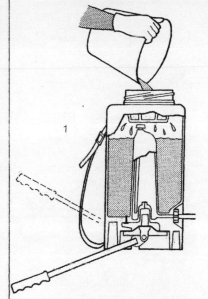

2. The lever is pulled up: The diaphragm is lowered; the water being drawn past valve A into the pressure cylindeer.

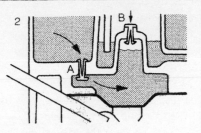

3. The lever is pushed down: The diaphragm is raised; the water being pushed up past valve B into the pressure chamber. (As one valve opens the other closes, thus driving the water one way all the time).

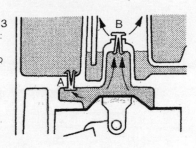

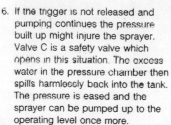

4. As more water enters the pressure chamber (p), the trapped air is compressed; it becomes slightly harder to work the pump handle. The experienced operator soon comes to know the feel of this moment.

5. Now the operator squeezes the trigger opening the valve attached to it. The compressed air releases like a spring and propels the water from the sprayer in a steady stream.

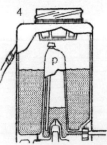

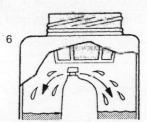

6. If the trigger is not released and pumping continues the pressure built up might injure the sprayer. Valve C is a safety valve which opens in this situation. The excess water in the pressure chamber then spills harmlessly back into the tank. The pressure is eased and the sprayer can be pumped up to the operating level once more.

Fig. 7.2 The water's passage through the sprayer

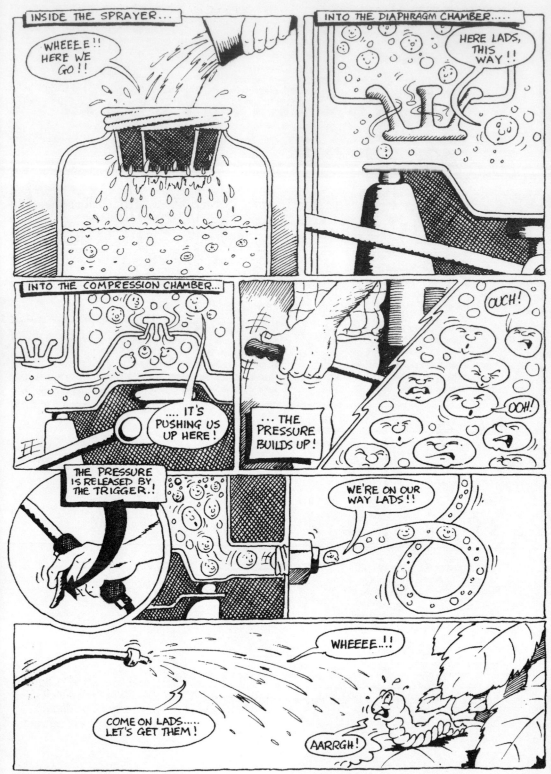

30

This assembly of parts is forced open if the lever is pumped for too long before the trigger is used. It prevents wear and tear on the pressure chamber and the hose connections.

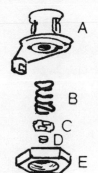

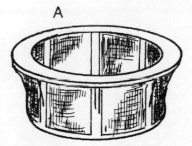

(a) The pressure adjuster has 2 positions, H (high) is for pesticides and L (low) is for herbicide (weed killers).

(b) The spring – is pushed up by excessive pressure.

(c) The holder – keeps the spring firmly in place.

(d) The disc – fits into the holder and closes/opens the system

(e) Screws down onto the relief body. It must be tight enough to compress the O ring, but not too tight.

(f) The relief body contains parts 2–4.

(g) The O ring prevents leaking if it is gently compressed.

(h) The spigot fits into the relief pipe

(i) The relief pipe reaches the bottom of the pressure chamber. When the relief valve opens water rushes up this pipe, past the disc and into the tank.

(j) The pressure chamber.

Fig. 7.3   An exploded diagram of the relief valve

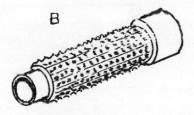

(b) The trigger valve filter is inside the filter barrel between the trigger valve and the hose. It protects the trigger valve and nozzle from clogging with particles that may have passed through the basket filter.

) The basket filter or strainer hangs in the neck of the tank. Everything poured into the tank must go through this filter.

Fig. 7.4   The filters

Parts that may have to be taken out and cleaned

Not every knapsack sprayer is exactly the same as the models described in this unit. The features that hold the diaphragm and produce the pressure, however, are all very similar in the leading makes.

The screw cap   (Fig. 7.6) closes the sprayer. It has a valve that admits air into the tank but does not let it out. This must be kept clear; check that it has not been blocked. Some models have a hole instead of a valve.

The basket filter   (Fig. 7.4a) prevents bits of leaf, insect bodies, sand and other impurities from entering the tank and clogging the valves. Never remove it when filling the tank. Pour slowly and stop to clear whenever necessary.

The lance filter   (Fig. 7.4b) is inside the lance just behind the trigger. Its mesh is finer than that of the basket filter. It catches particles that might have fallen through the first filter and into the tank. It protects the nozzle.

The suction and the pressure valves   (Figs 7.2, 7.6) force the liquid to flow in one direction. They are worked by water pressure and when one opens the other closes. The suction valve lets liquid from the tank flow into the pressure cylinder. The pressure valve lets liquid from the pressure cylinder flow into the pressure chamber. Both valves are located in the cylinder liner (Fig. 7.6). Be careful when removing them not to injure the liner, but manoeuvre the flanged legs so that they slip out of their holes without being forced.

The relief or safety valve   (Figs 7.2, 7.3) is a device which opens if too much liquid is forced into the pressure chamber. (This can happen either by over-pumping, working the lever too long without releasing the trigger, or if the nozzle is blocked.) To prevent high pressure from injuring the equipment the valve opens, liquid in the chamber spurts back into the tank, and the strain on the pressure chamber is relieved. Users quickly learn the 'feel' of the lever when the pressure is 'right' and the trigger can be operated.

The nozzle   (Figs 7.2, 7.5) breaks the liquid into a cone shaped spray that covers the crop. This task is carried out by three tiny parts inside the nozzle – the spray disc, swirl cone and gasket. If these are taken out they must be put back in the order shown or the spray cloud will not form and a jet, useless for spraying, will leak from the nozzle.

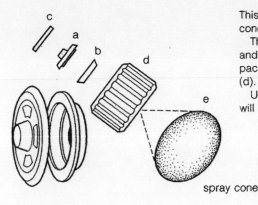

This nozzle produces a hollow cone with the spray concentrated at its outer edge.

The cone pattern is formed by the swirl plate (a) and the spray disc (b). The washer (c) serves to pack the parts tightly in place inside the nozzle cap (d).

Unless the three parts are in this order the water will not emerge as a cone of spray but as a jet.

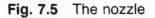

spray cone

Fig. 7.5 The nozzle

The diaphragm (Figs 7.2, 7.6, 7.8) is a flexible plastic disc moved up and down by a crank shaft attached to the lever. The lever's action alters the size of the pressure cylinder, the chamber that holds the diaphragm. It thus forces the liquid from the tank through to the nozzle. Very rarely the diaphragm might need changing. This can be done by the user. (See below – Taking your sprayer apart.) Replacement parts are sold either singly or in assembly packets of parts that go together. Be wary of buying sprayers for which it is unlikely that you can get spare parts because improvised parts seldom work as intended. They reduce the efficiency and shorten the life of the sprayer and are, at best, an interim solution to problems.

The crank (Fig. 7.7) grips the lower diaphragm holder (Fig. 7.8), and must be released when the diaphragm is taken out for inspection. Slide the bearings apart. This releases the crank which can then be unhooked from the holder. The bearings may, at this point, be cleaned and lubricated.

The cylinder liner assembly (Fig. 7.6) consists of the pressure cylinder (inside which the diaphragm works), and the cylinder liner, O ring and suction and pressure valves. In order to clean any of these the cylinder liner must be taken out of the pressure cylinder. Do this by pressing on the two cylinder liner projecting knobs. Once the cylinder liner is free the valves can be manoeuvred from their holes and cleaned if necessary. The O ring must be regularly greased so that it remains flexible and can be removed if necessary.

The nozzle (Figs 7.2, 7.5) shapes the spray into a cone and if it must be cleaned then the parts must be replaced in the order shown in the diagram or the spray-cone will not form. Nozzles, producing different spray patterns such as solid cones or strips, can be ordered. They are specialised and are generally used with herbicides.

Taking the sprayer apart

It is important, to do this in an organised manner so that you neither lose the pieces nor find them left over when you have reassembled the sprayer.

If you buy your sprayer from a recognised manufacturer's agent you will be shown how to take out the diaphragm and valves and check parts for wear or damage. Practice a few times after the demonstration. Some manufacturers organise demonstration days for agricultural agents at regional centres.

If possible take your sprayer apart, the first time, under the supervision of a trained instructor.

When you take your sprayer apart have ready a mat on which to place all the parts. As they come out place them on the mat in the order in which you remove them. When you are reassembling the equipment you simply work in reverse order.

As an example of the procedure a description follows of how to take out and disassemble the pressure cylinder and the cylinder lining so as to reach the valves or the diaphragm.

1. Slide the bearings apart, Fig. 7.7.
2. Unhook the crank, lay it on the mat.
3. Loosen the seven screws. The clamp ring will come away when they are unscrewed halfway and the assembly of screws, washers and clamp ring need not be taken apart further.
4. Draw out the diaphragm assembly. This consists of the upper and lower diaphragm holders with the diaphragm and pressure cylinder sandwiched between them. All are held together by the central screw.
5. If you wish to inspect or replace the diaphragm you now take out the central screw, lay it on the mat, separate the diaphragm and lay that down between the upper and lower diaphragm holders. It can now be examined or cleaned. (Fig. 7.8 shows this stage.)
6. If you wish only to inspect the valves you can leave the diaphragm assembly in one piece, but you will have to separate the cylinder lining from its protecting shell, the pressure cylinder. This is a delicate operation and must be done carefully. Turn the sprayer the right way up. Look into the tank and you will see two white knobs, one either side of the pressure cylinder (Fig. 7.6). Push on them gently with your thumbs or a screw driver and the liner will fall out of position. Lift the sprayer body and the liner is left underneath.
7. The liner holds the suction valve to one side and the pressure valve at the top. Lever out the valves by pressing on their flanged legs and

manoeuvring them gently through their holes. It is important not to scratch or injure the liner. Complete any necessary cleaning.

8. To change the O ring pull it out of its groove, clean, grease and replace it. A new O ring must also be greased before it is put in place. Make sure it is seated neatly in the groove.

Tracking down trouble

When parts need cleaning or replacing or are wrongly positioned the results may be low pressure (Fig. 7.6), leakage (Fig. 7.8), or a jammed, stiff-working lever (Fig. 7.7).

If parts need cleaning do it promptly because dirt fragments cause damage. If parts are damaged it is best to buy the manufacturer's replacement parts.

(a)

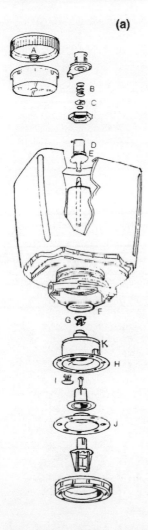

A   The air-hole or valve in the Screw-Cap may be blocked. Clear it.

B   The relief valve spring could be slack. Replace it.

C   The relief valve holder must seat the spring above and the disc below firmly. If the disc is pitted replace it.

D   The relief body – unlikely to need replacement.

E   The sealing washer may be perished. Replace it.

See Fig. 7.3

The cylinder liner

F   If the O ring is distorted or damaged replace it.

G   The inlet valve might be fouled or blocked. Clear it.

H   The cylinder liner may be distorted. Replace it.

K   The cylinder liner projecting knob. Press both to ease the liner out of the cylinder.

I   The outlet valve might be fouled, blocked or damaged. Clear or replace it.

J   The diaphragm may be cracked or worn. Replace it.

F to I are all part of the cylinder liner, and come out of the tank in a unit. This unit can be taken apart for cleaning or repair.

(b) VALVE

VALVE

Fig. 7.6 Causes of low pressure, failure to get a good spray cone

Only if these are unavailable should improvised ones be used and then only as an interim arrangement till the correct part can be obtained. Good maintenance will ensure that several years pass before replacement parts are needed.

Figs 7.6 to 7.8 are 'exploded' diagrams showing parts inside the sprayer as if they are pulled out in the order in which they fit into each other. Some parts shown one below the other, in fact fit inside each other.

Stiffness or jamming of the lever   If the lever will not move or moves stiffly the probable cause is blockage or clogging at valves A or B, or the lance filter Fig. 7.6.

Leaking at or near the base   This could originate in the diaphragm assembly (a), or in parts of the hose assembly (b).

(a)

A   The central screw might be loose. Tighten it.

B   The upper diaphragm holder.

C   The diaphragm is held in place by the clamp ring. If it is worn, buckled or cracked. Replace it.

D   The lower diaphragm holder fits on to the crank and lever.

E   The clamp ring.

F   7 screws fix the diaphragm. They must all be tight, with their washers (G) in place.

The crank (C), that works the diaphragm may not be firmly in place. Check this and see that the unit is clean.
The bearings may need lubricating and cleaning or replacing if they are damaged. Also;
If the washer (W) is worn replace it.
If the hose clips (HC) are slack tighten them and make sure they are securely in place.

(b)

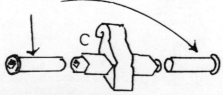

[Dip Tube O ring (Fig. 7.7), may be worn. Replace it].

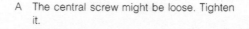

Fig. 7.7 a & b   Diaphragm assembly and clamp ring

Fig. 7.8   (Right)   Lever and crank connection

37

Safe spraying

When chemicals are being applied both environment and user must be protected. Unit 5 deals with environmental protection. Here we deal with the user's safety.

Any chemical that dehydrates (dries) insects or acts on their nervous system can, to a lesser extent, do the same to larger creatures, including man. The effects of poisoning, sickness, numbness and itching worsen with longer exposure to the chemical. Thus a splash of a pyrethroid wiped dry after a minute will have no effect, but a fine spray that wets the operator all morning during treatment of a crop may cause irritation that afternoon or later. The following rules for safe spraying must be observed for all chemicals, whether made on the farm or bought from shops.

1. Be aware of wind direction. Never spray so that you risk breathing in the spray (Fig. 7.9c). The nose is a very efficient filter and in the open field it is not very likely that drops will be inhaled into the lungs. Nevertheless always spray so that the wind carries the spray away from you.
2. Avoid walking through the spray cloud or though plants wet with spray (Fig. 7.9b). If clothes are wetted they keep the skin damp and irritate it by rubbing. The chemicals are, in fact, being rubbed into the skin. It is most important that cloths used as face masks be kept absolutely dry. If by chance one is wetted it must be removed at once; changed if possible, but removed in any case.
3. Spray close to the crop. The wind cannot then pick up the droplets and carry them to other workers nearby.
4. Mask the face with a cloth. Even in a light breeze tiny droplets hang in the air and can be breathed in (Fig. 7.9e).
5. Solutions mixed in a pail should be stirred with a stick, never with the hand (Fig. 7.9d). When mixing in the sprayer use the following procedure:
   - half fill the tank with clean water,
   - pour in the concentrate
   - top up the tank with clean water.
6. Wipe the outside of the tank dry before hoisting it onto the back (Fig. 7.9f).
7. After spraying, having emptied and washed out the tank (Fig. 7.10a), wash your hands and face in clean water. Never smoke or eat before having washed thoroughly. Chemicals can be carried to the mouth and even though the amounts are small, they can accumulate, causing sickness later.

8. After the tank has been emptied clean water must be pumped through it to clean the hose, lance and nozzle of all chemicals.
9. Store the tank upside down, on a high shelf out of reach of animals and children (Fig. 7.10b).
10. Keep all vessels in which chemicals are mixed separate for that purpose only. Store them beside the tank (Fig. 7.10c). Make sure that everyone knows they are for use only with poisons.
11. Few village-available chemicals are stable so concentrated solutions cannot usually be stored, but if synthetic pesticides, or powders or dusted seeds are stored make sure they are labelled. The outline of a skull (Fig. 7.10d) indicates that the contents of a container are dangerous. (Sodium bicarbonate, a fungicide mentioned in Unit 14, is not poisonous. Small amounts are used in baking and to relieve indigestion.)

Table 7.1 Characteristics of some insecticides, commercial or village-available

Common name	Description	Supplied as
Dieldrin	Synthetic, broad-spectrum, very toxic (poisonous). Very persistent. Safe to bees.	Emulsion, wettable powder, dust, grains.
DDT	Synthetic, broad spectrum, very toxic, very persistent. Pre-harvest interval 2 weeks. Banned in Europe.	Emulsion, wettable powder, dust, liquid.
Malathion	Synthetic, broad-spectrum, moderately toxic, persists up to 7 days.	Emulsion, wettable powder, dusts.
Carbaryl	Synthetic, broad-spectrum, moderately toxic, very persistent.	Wettable powder, dusts.
Fenitrothion	Synthetic, broad-spectrum, very toxic, persistent. Pre-harvest interval 1 week.	Emulsion, wettable powder, dusts.
Pyrethrin	Plant extract, broad-spectrum, very toxic, low resistance, Pre-harvest interval 1 day. Contact insecticide.	Dusts, or village-available infusions.
Rotenone	Plant extract, selective, moderately toxic, low persistence, Pre-harvest interval 1 day.	Dusts, or village-available infusions.
Nicotine	Plant extract, broad-spectrum, very toxic, very low persistence. Pre-harvest interval 2 days.	Infusion of cigarette or of fresh tobacco leaves.
Detergents	Fatty acids compounded with metallic salts, broad spectrum, non-toxic. Acts only while wet. Test first.	Concentrated liquids, powders. Village-available.
Neem Oil	Plant extract. broad-spectrum, low persistence, moderate toxicity.	Aerosol, or village-available infusions or powder.

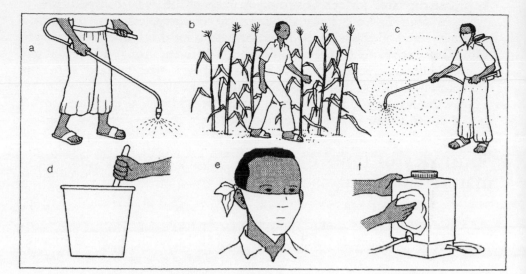

Fig. 7.9 Safety while spraying pesticides

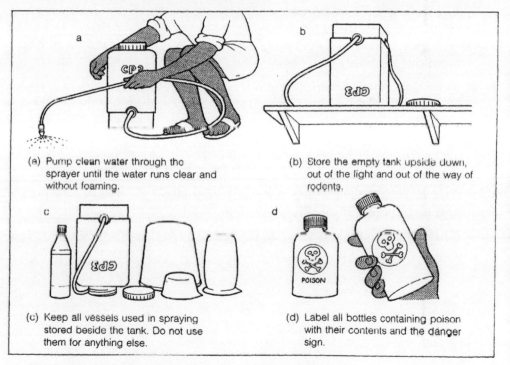

(a) Pump clean water through the sprayer until the water runs clear and without foaming.

(b) Store the empty tank upside down, out of the light and out of the way of rodents.

(c) Keep all vessels used in spraying stored beside the tank. Do not use them for anything else.

(d) Label all bottles containing poison with their contents and the danger sign.

Fig. 7.10 Safe storage of chemicals and equipment

Application rates Many governments restrict the import of pesticides to a chosen few. These are tested within the country, often at the central university, and on the basis of this information local Departments of Agriculture can recommend application rates for different crops and regions and for small acreages. Rates are printed on the label as litres/hectare. A hectare is 2.5 acres or 10,000 (ten thousand), square metres.

Growers in any doubt as to how much of a chemical is proper to use should consult their nearest Extension Officer.

Summary of units 6 and 7 Spray equipment, its maintenance and use

1. Unmechanised hydraulic sprayers, worked by diaphragm pumps, are relatively inexpensive and are designed to be serviced and maintained by the user.

2. They are safer to use than hydraulic sprayers fitted with piston pumps.

3. Growers who cannot get these or who are treating very small plots can improvise with twigs or plastic-bottle sprays provided that only harmless sprays such as soap, disinfectant solution or sodium bicarbonate solutions are used.

4. Treat your sprayer with care and it will give you many years of service. If you must disassemble it for inspection or cleaning use the following procedure:
   As you take your sprayer to pieces lay the parts down on a clean surface in the order they were removed from the equipment. When reassembling the equipment put them back in reverse order.

5. The rules of safe spraying and consideration for the health of the user and neighbours, must always be observed.

6. The rules for safe and separate storage of pesticides and the dishes and bowls in which they are mixed must always be observed.

CHEMICALS AND TRAPS FOR PEST CONTROL

UNIT 8 Introducing village-available insecticides

When, despite all care, pest outbreaks occur, insecticides can be bought to protect crops and family income. The units that follow give information to guide buyers – but insecticides can also be made on the farm from local plants or from ingredients sold in ordinary village shops. These are the village-available insecticides.

Commercially available pesticides

These come in various forms.

- Concentrated liquids which must be diluted.
- Oil/water emulsions which separate unless mixed vigorously.
- Wettable powders which must be agitated gently during spraying.
- Dusts generally used to dress seeds before planting, or sometimes packed so that a cloud of fine dust can be 'puffed' out.

Though a few pesticides are plant based most are synthetic, created in laboratories from oil and coal. Their persistence (how long they stay active) depends on the chemicals used and the manufacturers' design. Their safety to people depends on how they are used. (Unit 7 must be read in conjunction with the material in this section.) Most are broad-spectrum, which means they act on many different insects.

Integrated Pest Management (Unit 5), recommends that insecticides must kill pests and leave untouched other insects. This seems an impossible demand. Any field has in it hundreds of flies, caterpillars and spiders hidden among the leaves or under the soil, all of whom are at risk from the spray. However, although the insecticides described in these units are all wide spectrum killers, they are not all equally persistent. Used with care, they fulfil the demands of IPM to kill mainly the target pests.

Village-available pesticides

These are inevitably cheaper than commercially supplied formulations. Pesticides can amount to a large part of a growers' expenses. Economy, however, is not the only advantage that follows from making your own insecticides on the farm. There is also the fact that, should supplies of commercial insecticides fail or should pests in the region develop resistance to the compounds on sale, growers have recourse to substances that can be relied on. Also these natural extracts do not appear to induce resistance, they often contain more than one poison and each acts in its own way. The disadvantages are that it takes time and skill to make your own sprays and dusts and some of these mixtures must be 'test sprayed' before use. Growers have much to gain, however, from experimenting and learning how to use locally made insecticides.

Some village-available compounds are made from plants, some from minerals and some are animal products. Over the last half-century of research more than a thousand insecticidal plant varieties have been found, and there may be others not yet recorded. Elders and medicine men who know local plants could have suggestions worth testing.

Methods of making these medicines are familiar to any housewife, but in science the following terms describe the different procedures.

Infusions are made by bringing water to the boil, then removing it from the heat. The plant parts are immersed, either whole, cut or pounded, in the hot water and left until the water has cooled.

Macerating means leaving the plant parts, usually bruised or ground to a powder, soaking for some hours in cold water.

Extracts are made by pressing the juice from plants and diluting it with clean water.

Bruising means lightly pounding fresh plant parts in a mortar. This speeds the release of plant chemicals, thus making macerating more effective.

Dusts are fine powders, pounded thoroughly in a mortar.

Nicotine insecticide

This chemical has been used for over a hundred years to kill insect pests. It is a powerful nerve poison extracted from the tobacco plant (Fig. 8.1). It kills insects by contact, also if inhaled or eaten. In parts of West Africa the herb is interplanted with maize because it is said to lower the numbers of borer insects on the maize. Nicotine kills aphids, thrips and caterpillars and the eggs of butterflies and moths. It is extremely poisonous to all livestock, both cattle and poultry. It can kill people. The nicotine of half a cigarette is enough to kill a full grown man so the user must not breathe in the spray or wet the skin or clothes in the liquid. Children must not be allowed near when it is being prepared or used. The bowls or other vessels in which it is made must be kept separate and never used to prepare food.

Nicotine insecticide can be prepared from fresh leaves or cigarettes. It can be infused or macerated (Fig. 8.1). In India tobacco dust was used to dress seed for planting and gave good protection. The dust keeps its poison properties much longer than does the water extract. Do not use it to dust plants intended for eating, nor store it near food. When made as a spray nicotine persists for two to three days, then it breaks down and disappears. After that interval sprayed crops can be eaten or taken to market and cattle can graze treated grasses or leaves.

It is curious that aphids, readily killed by nicotine, should yet infest the tobacco plant. This is because the insect sucks sap from the phloem cells that carry sugars to and from the leaves, while the nicotine is found only in the xylem cells that carry water from the roots.

left: Soak 1 cigarette, or 10–15 leaves, in hot water for ten minutes, *right* or soak them overnight in cold water.

Filter the liquid into the tank.

Stir in a small handful of soap.

Half fill the tank with clean, cold water.

Fig. 8.1 Preparing nicotine insecticide spray (10 litres)

UNIT 9 More village-available insecticides

Neem

The neem is a fast growing tree orig-
inally from the Indian sub-continent
but now found in all parts of Africa.
It contains several insecticidal compounds. The main one, azadiractin,
both deters and also kills many serious
insect pests. A company has recently
started to market neem spray in an
aerosol can. Packed in that way it is
too expensive for agricultural use but
the opportunity exists for small indus-
tries to sell the cleaned, dried seeds or
leaves together with instructions for
making the spray. Stored in darkness

the seeds keep their killing power for a year. Neem grows well in poor
soils and where the rainfall is as low as 250 mm a year. The water table
should not be much over 5 m from the surface. If pruned it quickly puts
out more leaves and gives a denser shade than if left to spread naturally,
but its seed production is reduced. Growers who wish to produce seed for
sale in addition to supplying their own insecticide needs, will let the tree
grow without pruning or will prune lightly after the seeds have fallen. The
seeds stay alive for only two weeks after falling so the grower who wants
a plantation of this useful tree must clean off the mealy covering of the ripe
fruits and plant the seeds without delay. They should be planted in well
drained, sandy soil or in pots for later transplanting.

Neem oil discourages insects from feeding. Scientists have observed
insects, unable to feed, wandering about on sprayed leaves till they starve.
The oil has other properties; females will not lay their eggs on sprayed
leaves. Though insects hit by the spray do not always die instantly and may
even recover and lay eggs, the pupae are malformed and the adults never
emerge. The oil is effective against a long list of chewing and boring pests.
Every part of the plant contains the oil but the seeds are richest in it. Both
seeds and leaves are widely used in India. Powdered, they are dusted over
grain stored for planting. The dust must not be stored near food or used
to treat grain intended for eating. Infused or macerated the leaves and seeds
make a spray (Fig. 9.1).

The effective chemicals in neem oil break down in sunlight so killing
rates are highest if the infusion is made under shade and applied in the
evening. This ensures its usefulness against night flying insects such as the
moth of the tomato fruit worm. The liquid can be stored in the dark for
3–4 days without losing its insecticidal properties but after 7 days in sunlight

neem has lost 50% of its killing power. The seeds should be cleaned of their mealy coating and stored in darkness. They can be prepared as needed. A powder of pounded seeds can be used to dust grain intended for planting. Mixed with the soil the powder protects plants against nematodes.

Though poorer in oil than the seeds, the leaves have the advantage of being available all year and in India are traditionally used to protect stored grain intended for eating. For this purpose they are not powdered but just thrown whole, in layers or at random, into village grain stores. The rates used are 2–5 kg dry leaves to 100 kg of grain.

Crush 2 handfuls of seeds to a coarse powder or bruise 1 kg of leaves. To make a concentrate;

Infuse them 15 minutes in hot water or overnight in cold water.

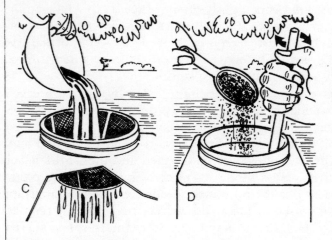

Working under shade filter the concentrate into a half filled tank. Stir in a little soap powder and top up the tank with clean, cold water.

Spray the crop in the late afternoon because neem breaks down in sunlight.

Fig. 9.1 Preparing an insecticidal spray from neem

Pyrethrum

Pyrethrum is a daisy-like chrysanthemum from the Mediterranean that was introduced into Africa at the turn of the century. Only the open flower heads contain the insecticide – pyrethrin.

In order to develop its flowers pyrethrum needs cool temperatures, rainfall of around 1200 mm and dry weather while the flowers are developing. It can withstand 12° of frost. In the tropics it must be grown from 1600 to 3000 metres above sea level. The flowerheads develop more pyrethrin when they are fertilised, so insecticides that harm pollinating insects will also lower the value of the crop.

The principal active ingredient, pyrethrin, is a nerve poison. In low concentrations it does not kill but has a 'knock down' effect; that is, it first produces erratic movement in the victim and finally a paralysis from which insects recover inside 24 hours. Stronger doses kill.

- It breaks down in sunlight, though research has found ways of slowing down this reaction and commercial formulations are more persistent than those made on the farm.
- It can be used as a dust by powdering the flowerheads. This dust may be stored in darkness and infused later to make the spray.
- The spray is made by infusing or macerating the flowerheads. The liquid should be applied soon after making, preferably in the evening when the light is no longer intense.
- Unlike neem its effects on warm-blooded animals are so slight that it is regarded as non-poisonous and can be used to dust grain that will later be eaten, or to treat meat or fish being dried in the open.
- Commercially it is sold in powder form.

Pyrethrin is harmless to honey bees, animals, birds and people. This makes it especially useful in the home against fleas and lice. It is used to protect fish and meat during sun-drying. Pyrethrin kills flies before they can lay their eggs on the surface sprayed. Keep the powder out of the reach of children. It is an irritant and can cause a rash after prolonged exposure. Breathing the dust can cause headaches and sickness.

The pyrethroids Scientists have developed synthetic (man-made), substances similar to pyrethrin. These are the pyrethroids. They are marketed under various trade names (Ambush, Decis), and are different in a number of ways from the natural product. They are poisonous to honey bees and fish. Sun-light does not break them down and they 'stick' to leaf surfaces for weeks killing any insects that touch the leaves. This makes them less specific in action and more harmful to the environment than natural pyrethrin. In addition they irritate the skin. This irritation is a prickly feeling felt when the skin or eyes of users are rubbed. Pyrethroids can repel or kill depending on how strong a solution is mixed.

Other chrysanthemum species commonly called marigolds contain insecticides and insect repellents. The Mexican marigold, *Tagetes erecta*, is sometimes interplanted with crops in Britain and might well be examined in a tropical context.

Derris

Derris is a woody vine that grows in the humid tropics, and rotenone, a contact and stomach poison, is extracted from its roots. it is traded world wide. Rotenone is toxic (poisonous) to fish, pigs and honey bees. It is a skin irritant and if inhaled can give rise to a numb feeling in the lips, tongue and throat. The roots of wild vines contain 0.5% of rotenone but growers have developed varieties that yield up to 13% of their weight in the chemical.

Seeds remain viable (able to germinate) for up to six months. Before planting the seed coat must be nicked or lightly grazed so that moisture can enter the seed. It is quicker to grow derris from stem cuttings. These must be around 30cm long with at least three nodes. They are rooted in nursery beds and transplanted to the field after six weeks. At harvest the roots must be at least 2cm thick. This takes eight months if the vines are grown in sunlight and about 2 years in shade conditions.

After harvest the derris roots are dried to 10% of fresh weight and then stored in cool, dry darkness otherwise the chemical breaks down. Rotenone has very low persistence so once the spray is prepared it must be used at once. Stoll (1986) gives the following instructions for making the extract.

- Freshly cut roots 2–6 cm in diameter are washed and cut into 5 cm lengths. They are pounded, together with soap and a little water. When the roots are completely shredded into fibre the liquid is filtered off through a fine cloth. The resulting solution is diluted and used at once. The quantities recommended are:
  1 part soap: 4 parts roots: 225 parts water.
  In a 20 litre sprayer this approximates as:
  100 ml soap: 400 gm cut roots: 22 litres water or
  One teaglass soap: 4 teaglasses cut roots: one full tank of water.

Rotenone persists for not more than three days in the field but an interval of two weeks is recommended between the last application and taking the sprayed crop to market or into the kitchen.

It is effective against young grubs and larvae, aphids and spider mites. It is dangerous to fish (traditionally it was used in Borneo to paralyse fish during fish spearing expeditions), and very toxic to pigs.

Research has found ways to stabilise rotenone so commercial formulations last longer (are more stable), in the field than the village-made sprays. Manufacturers' directions as to dosage and safe intervals between the last application and harvest must be carefully followed. If the product is not sold in its original packet or if the grower has any doubts about the product he must consult his nearest Agricultural Extension Officer.

51

Other insecticidal plants

Hyptis spicigera is a herb that grows wild throughout Africa. Farmers in West Africa leave it if they find it growing among their crops. They believe its strong smell deters leaf chewing insects. Its leaves can be spread in grain stores.

Guiera senegalensis (Fig. 9.2) is a small tree that grows in arid Africa. Its seeds are sold as medicine and if locusts become a threat bunches of its leaves are burned in the fields because the pungent smoke is said to deter locusts. The effectiveness of this treatment has not been confirmed.

Euphorbia balsamifera is a woody succulent often used as a hedge. When wounded it oozes a latex which is said to be insecticidal. Animals do not find the plant palatable.

Lantana camera a weed with bright orange and yellow flowers, sometimes used as a garden ornamental in arid parts of Africa contains insecticides in its seeds and leaves.

Annona **species** (Fig 9.3a) soursop, sweetsop and custard apple are trees native to South America but grown in other continents for their edible fruits which are widely exported. Insecticides are found in all parts of the trees, except the ripe fruits. Field trials of the crude extracts might well be carried out by students, landowners or fortunately placed agricultural agents.

Chillipepper Ripe fruits and seeds contain the insecticidal compounds. The powder is highly irritant and difficult to work with, but good results are reported from Kenya on control of aphids in vegetable gardens. In Kenya the spray is prepared as follows:
   Ground chillies are soaked overnight in cold water and after filtering the solution is sprayed onto the plants.
   In the Philippines soap is added to the solution. The mixture should be test sprayed on a few plants a day before spraying the crop. Apply once a week if there is no rain; two or three times a weeks if it rains. Some investigation into chillipepper insecticides has been carried out at the University of Hawaii.

Garlic has also been investigated as an insecticide at the University of Hawaii. Gardeners in Germany use a water extract of garlic against pests. They recommend it be used immediately after making. The preparation is as follows:

• 100 garlic cloves, 0.5 l water, 10 g of soap, 2 teaspoons of kerosine. Steep the garlic in the kerosine for 24 hours. Add the soap and water. Stir well and filter through a cloth. For use dilute this solution with

10 l of water (half of a knapsack sprayer). There are about 10 cloves in a head but even so in many countries the price of garlic makes this recipe expensive.

Combretum micanthrum (Fig. 9.3b) is a tree of arid West Africa whose seeds are used as medicine and whose branches are woven into the walls of huts as an insect repellant.

Fig. 9.2 *Guiera senegalensis*

Fig. 9.3 The custard apple (*Annona sp*). (Left)

Combretum micanthrum (Right)

UNIT 10   Soaps, oils and disinfectants

In this book soap can be taken to mean both the soft soaps and the more easily bought washing powders and liquid detergents. Both types of compound can kill insects on contact. Depending on concentration soaps have three distinct and separate uses in spray programs.

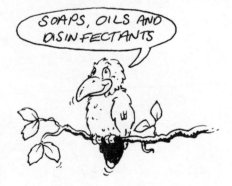

Soaps are complex mixtures of fats or oils with alkalis (soda or potash), and metallic salts. They seem to destroy insect membranes. Small insects, such as aphids, die instantly. Soaps and detergents are harmless to animals, birds and people.

For many years gardeners have known that soap and water kills insects, but because the mixtures sometimes damage plants users have to be careful. Research has isolated some of the insecticidal compounds in soap and they are now sold as insecticidal soaps, non-injurious to plants. These commercial packs are expensive and of little interest to farmers. Soaps act as insecticides at concentrations under 1% but at higher concentrations can injure plants. Care should be taken when making the solutions.

Soaps

These have three uses, depending on concentration.

1. In low concentrations (a pinch in the spray tank) soaps reduce surface tension so that water-drops spread flatly (Fig. 10.1). This brings any pesticide carried by the drops into close contact with the leaf surface. It also helps to spread the chemical evenly over target insects (those the grower wishes to kill). In this way soaps improve the power of all poison sprays. In addition they make mixing easier by aiding the dispersal of other substances, powder or liquid, into the water.
2. In concentrations from 0.5% to 0.8% (5–8 g per litre) they kill insects. At 0.5% death is instantaneous for aphids and small caterpillars. Large caterpillars and beetles need strengths of around 0.8%. Table 10.1 shows how to make these concentrations both with liquid and powdered soaps.
3. High concentrations (over 1%), damage or kill plants. Growers use them as herbicides (weed killers).

Soaps kill only while wet, once dry they lose their insecticide action. This limits their action to insects hit at the time of spraying. Thus solutions made to the right strength are, in effect, specific to the target insect, provided the user sprays carefully.

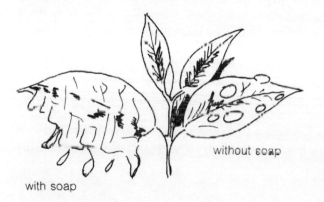

without soap

with soap

Fig. 10.1 The 'spreading effect' of soap

Vegetable oils

Vegetable oils are deterrents, as insects avoid their smell. A thin coating of the oils from peanut, cotton-seed, coconut, mustardseed, maize or soy-bean protects grain and other seeds from weevils and seed boring beetles. It is not completely clear how this works but both eggs and larvae die among grains so treated and the result is clean seed.

It is important to note that the oils reduce the ability of the grain to germinate, so grain intended for growing cannot be protected in this way. It can, however, be an efficient way for housewives to protect their kitchen stores. The amount of oil needed is small.

- 5 ml of peanut oil mixed in 1 kg of cowpeas protects for about 180 days.
- 6 ml of cottonseed oil mixed in 1 kg of mung beans protects for 3 months

The method of application is as follows: Pour the oil over the beans and stir thoroughly. If large family grain-stores are being protected it might be easier to spray the oils with the help of a plastic bottle (Fig. 6.2). Stir the grain to distribute the oil evenly.

Disinfectants (Antiseptics)

Growers can improve the insecticidal power of a soap and water solution by adding a few millilitres of disinfectant. These retard or stop the growth of bacteria (Unit 13).

There is an enormous variety of disinfectant compounds. They are used in clinics and hospitals to clean working surfaces and surgical instruments, and around the home to clean cuts and abrasions. Some are sold as mouth-wash and can be gargled with. These liquids are usually sold along with soaps. They come in various colours and scents which make them agreeable to use and easy to recognise.

There are also abrasive powder cleaners, iodine in solution or crystal form, bleaches and potassium permanganate crystals. All are usually sold as concentrates with instructions to dilute with water before using. They are dangerous and must be kept well out of the way of children.

Bactericidal compounds are sometimes found in plants, garlic is an example. Some are of mineral origin (potassium permanganate and iodine). Some, such as benzoic acid, found in pine trees, are made synthetically in laboratories. Their effect on insects is little known but many are powerful oxidants.

Heat and ultra-violet light are also antiseptic.

Table 10.1 Mixing soap and water

To use this table.

1. Decide which size container you will use.
2. Look down that column till you find the strength of solution you need; marked as follows

   (a) • Kills large insects like beetles, moths, caterpillars, etc.
   (b) •• Kills only small insects like aphids, thrips, greenfly, etc.

3. Look left along that line to the measures section. That will tell you how many handfuls, tea-glasses or millilitres you need to make that strength of solution.

Measures			Containers		
teaglasses tg	millilitres ml	handfuls; (m=man w=woman)	bucket 10 litres	sprayer 15 litres	sprayer 20 litres
2	200	4m–6w	2.0% soln	1.5% soln	•1.0% soln
1½	150	3m–4½w	1.5% soln	•1.0% soln	•0.8% soln
1	100	2m–3w	•1.0% soln	•0.8% soln	••0.5% soln
⅘	80	1½m–2w	•0.8% soln	••0.6% soln	••0.4% soln
½	50	1m–1½w	••0.6% soln	••0.4% soln	••0.3% soln

Concentrations below 0.4% are unlikely to have any significant insecticidal action and concentrations over 1.0% might injure some crops.

'Kitchen measures' are convenient to use in the field. They can be made up by anyone with access to measuring glasses. Agents should work out how much liquid or powder are contained in household objects such as plastic bottles and tins and effectively make their own 'kitchen measures.' The measures used in the above table are based on the following facts.

A tea-spoon (small spoon) holds 2.5 ml of liquid or 0.5 gm powder
A table-spoon (large spoon), holds 5.0 ml of liquid or 1 gm powder
A ¾ full teaglass (Fig 14.1) holds 100 ml of liquid or 40 gm of powder.
A handful is a pile that fills the open palm (Fig 14.2)

Additions: A few drops of disinfectant enhances the killing power of soap solutions. These preparations are all very different so any mixture must be tried on a few plants before spraying the crop. The day before spraying apply the solution you have made up to one or two plants. If no damage has appeared by the following day it is safe to spray the crop with that solution.

Building a data base

It will add to local and regional knowledge to note the following facts when village-available or commercially obtained sprays are used.

The date made. . . .
The date used. . . .
The container used, (bucket, small sprayer, etc.). . . .
The plant, or commercial product used. . . .
The amount of insecticide (handfuls, tea-glasses, grams, millilitres). . . .
The make of soap (if used). . . .
The make of disinfectant or household cleaner (if used). . . .
The amount, (teaspoons, tablespoons, millilitres). . . .
Weather conditions, (whether windy, bright or overcast, damp or dry). If possible note the temperature.
The success of the operation. 'Success' does not mean that every single pest insect in the field was killed. It means that the pest population fell below the point of economic importance. (Any damage done to the crop was so small as not to be important.) A few aphids or leaf chewing caterpillars are good and necessary. Their presence encourages insect-eating birds to remain in the field. After a successful spray operation inspection, 'rubbing off' and weeding should keep pest numbers down.

Setting a light trap (a lamp standing in a bowl of water) in the field overnight can help a farmer monitor the moths and judge whether it is time to spray. Monitoring (checking by count) the night catch throughout the year gives a good idea of the level at which the pest population numbers will mean economic loss. Several farmers, children, school classes all monitoring light traps can build up a useful picture of how pest populations swell and shrink with the changing seasons.

59

UNIT 11 Mineral and animal based insecticides

Village-available chemicals can, like synthetic compounds, either kill or deter pests. The population of any pest prevented from laying or feeding will decline. The gritty dusts described here act as either deterrents or killers depending on how they are used.

Minerals

Laterite the common red soil of the arid tropics, when finely crushed protects stored grain and beans. In family grain stores (Fig. 11.1), or in sealed clay pots, the dust deters insects from boring into or laying their eggs on the dusted grain. Laterite rubs the waterproof waxy coating off insect bodies and they dehydrate. Insects instinctively avoid abrasive surfaces of that kind.

In sealed storage pots insects suffocate because enough dust is poured in with the grain to exclude air. Also, trapped insects dehydrate and die if their outer coating is damaged by abrasion. Dust affords some protection to leaves but it washes off easily and does not stick well to the underside, so pests that shelter there are not deterred.

Ash from the remains of cooking fires, can protect leaves from chewing insects. The ashes must be crushed, then thinly and evenly spread. This can be done by putting them into a coarse textured bag which is shaken over the crop (Fig. 11.2). Ashes provide more protection in the dry than in the rainy season. When washed off the leaves they fertilise the soil very effectively.

Fuel oil and kerosine kill plants as well as insects but are useful against insects that congregate. Nests of leaf curling ants can be dipped. The oil kills them in seconds; spent motor oil is useful for this operation. The oil is very flammable. Do not smoke or bring any flame near it.

Animal product pesticides

Fermented cow urine makes an effective spray against all kinds of insects. It can be readily collected from penned cattle if the ground is made to slope slightly towards a pit or trough. The urine runs into the pit leaving the dung on the ground. The liquid must be kept a few days to ferment, and this is best done in full sun. Before use dilute 1 part urine to 6 parts water. Filter through a coarse cloth before pouring it through the basket filter into the sprayer.

Fig. 11.1 A village grain store (left)

Fig. 11.2 Dusting crops with pounded ashes (right)

Summary of units 8 to 11   Insecticides

1. Pesticides are not exclusively factory made. Many powerful insecticides are the natural products of plants and can be extracted on the farm by simple methods such as soaking and crushing.
2. Insecticidal plants include tobacco and neem which will grow in semi-arid or moist tropical climates. Derris which grows in the wet tropics and yields rotenone and pyrethrum which grows at high altitudes in the semi-arid tropics are also used.
3. Soaps and detergents, both liquid and powdered, are effective insect killers, though at concentrations of 1% and over they harm some plants. Disinfectants kill insects too. Test these solutions on a few plants before spraying the whole crop.
4. A thin coat of vegetable oil protects grain from weevils. It prevents germination so is useful only for grain intended for eating.
5. Minerals (dusts and ashes) and urine collected from penned animals and diluted 1 part urine to 6 parts water, also make effective insecticides.
6. Some other plants found to contain insecticides are listed. Growers and agents should test likely local medicinal plants.
7. Most insecticides are to some extent harmful to mammals including man. Use them with the precautions outlined in Unit 7.
8. Good pest control does not mean eradication. A few insects of the pest variety in a field are natural and necessary otherwise their predators will not remain.

UNIT 12   Other small pests

Many creatures like our edible crops. If the damage they do is characteristic and the creature can be identified then traps and baits can be set, or other action taken. If the wounds they make are invaded by bacteria, fungi or viruses the original cause may go undiscovered. It helps if the creature responsible is found nearby. If only damaged plants are found growers must be able to make an intelligent guess as to the cause. Remedies depend on our knowing the pest and its habits.

Nematodes

Nematodes are microscopic worms (sometimes called eel-worms), that live in the soil. Most live on dead plant materials (these are saprophytes), but a few (parasites), take food and water from living plants. Nematodes lay their eggs free in the soil or attached to roots. When the young parasites hatch they move to a host plant. They never move far so nematode infections generally cover only a small part of any field.

Nematodes attack a wide range of crops through leaves, buds and roots. By far the most serious pests are the *Meloidogyne* species which attack roots both by sucking the cell sap and by admitting pathogens through the wounds they have made. Some plant families are more at risk than others, so the worms can be controlled by crop rotation, see below.

They can be a long-term problem among trees. Some tree species, for example *Prosopis*, are known to harbour the worms. The parasites do not seem to harm the tree but can infect crops nearby. The eggs can cling to seed coats.

A nematode infection is hard to differentiate from some fungal diseases but if single plants start to wilt and die, dig them up and examine the roots. These will be malformed either by numerous swellings and bulges or by many individual lumps the size of a pin head. (The two types of malformation are caused by different species.) Control can be effected in the following ways:

1. Clean seeds   Seeds suspected of coming from infected fields should be given the following hot water treatment:

- make a bag out of some cheap, thin cloth.
- fill it half full of seeds.
- dip it in warm water; this gets rid of air bubbles.

- then dip it into hot water and keep it immersed and moving around for 25 minutes.
- water temperature must be an accurate 50°C. Check with a thermometer. This treatment also kills many fungal spores. Though this treatment kills many types of eel-worm it does not unfortunately, kill root-knot nematodes.

2. Clean cuttings or transplants   Dip root or stem sections in a cold infusion of garlic or neem (Unit 9), for 20 to 30 minutes. Neem is listed as a nematicide at theNatural Resources Institute of the University of Hawaii.

3. Resistant crop varieties   have been developed but as they are resistant usually to only one type of nematode this will not help a farmer whose fields are infested by another type.

4. Rotate crops   Nematodes do not travel far from their host but if the same crops are planted year after year, without break in the same bed, the worms will spread slowly until the entire field is infected. They cannot parasitise roots of grasses or alliums (The onion family), so a rotation that includes such crops leaves the worms with nothing to feed on. Their numbers are reduced through starvation. If *Prosopis* trees are used as hedges or shade trees particular care must be taken to maintain a good crop rotation.

5. Crop hygiene   Dig up affected plants and burn them as soon as possible.

6. Bare fallowing   is advisable if a field is infected over a large area and for any reason grain crops or grasses cannot be sown. At the start of the dry season plough deeply; then keep the field free of all growth till the following rains.

7. An infusion of quassia wood-chips   kills soil nematodes but cannot be used on edible crops as the chemical, quassin, is systemic (it enters the plant's sap stream), and infects fruit and leaves with a bitter taste.

8. The synthetic nematicides   in most general use are soil fumigants. They are applied with an injector or from a pressurised can. They are fatal if inhaled and more suited to use in experiment stations than in general agriculture. They must never be applied save by an experienced operator.

Snails

Snails (Fig. 12.1a), and slugs, (which are in the same family group but have no shells) inhabit damp, shady sites and swamps and can be numerous in the rainy season. They live in holes, coming out to graze at night. They cause little damage to mature plants, but if they invade a nursery or chew young shoots, they can do economically important harm. To stop snails invading nursery beds the following are recommended:

- Surround the bed with a 'barrier strip' of ash or dry grit.
- When irrigating keep the area round the bed dry.
- Snails inside the bed can be picked off at night by torchlight.
- Individual seedlings can be guarded by plastic bottles with both ends cut off, slipped over the stem. (Fig. 12.1b)

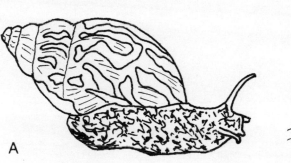

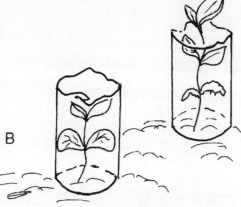

A

B

(a) The giant African snail.

(b) Protection for individual plants against snails and slugs.

Fig. 12.1 Snails

Birds

Birds are the growers' allies since they eat more insects than seeds, but seed eating birds that live in colonies, for example queleas, weavers and sparrows, often cause considerable damage to grain crops. Maize is seldom attacked because of the size of the seed, but millet and sorghum are taken. Some varieties are protected by unusually tough husks or a bitter taste but popular edible varieties are at risk.

'Goose necked' sorghum varieties bend their ripening heads at an angle that makes it difficult for birds to reach the grain. In West Africa farmers go through the sorghum when it is nearly ripe, bending the heads over.

Weaver birds strip leaves to make their nests, bananas are particularly at risk.

Bird scarers Growers use a variety of mechanical devices to frighten birds from the fields. Strings hung with objects that flutter and glitter in the wind are stretched over the crops. Scarecrows, man-like figures dressed in fluttering rags are put here and there in the field. Sometimes strings are

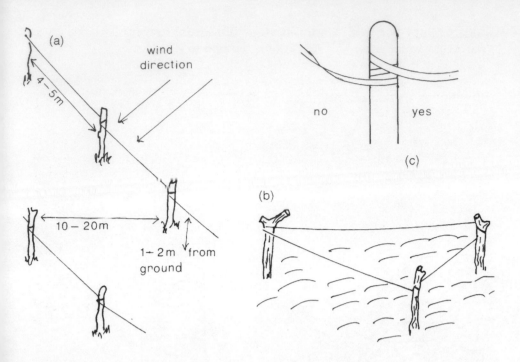

If the wind comes mainly from one direction use the plan shown in (a), but if winds are variable the plan shown in (b) is better. Be careful when staking, not to twist the tape (c). Pull it taut enough to hear its 'hum'.

Fig. 12.2 Humming tape

hung with cans filled with little stones or strung with bottle caps that clatter when jerked by the child on watch. Noise-makers can be bought that let off a sound like gun-shot every few minutes. All these methods disturb and reduce feeding, but birds soon become accustomed to the devices.

The humming tape (Fig. 12.2) is a relatively new product that works well over newly sown seedbeds and low growing crops. Plastic tape vibrates in a light breeze and 'hums'. The noise varies from a soft flutter to a loud drumming sound depending on the windspeed and birds to not seem to grow used to the sound so quickly. More studies are needed before this can be said with certainty.

The tape used must be:

- light in weight and have great tensile strength (not break when pulled).
- sturdy enough to stay tightly stretched even if shaken by the wind over many weeks.
- about 5 mm wide.
- cassette or video tapes work well and will hum even though their tensile strength is less than that of special 'bird-scarer' tape, meaning that after 5 or 6 weeks they slacken and cease to give off any noise. Their 'hum'

is not so loud as that of humming tape but birds' hearing is more acute than ours.

To set up a humming tape

- stretch the tape at right angles to the prevailing wind or at various angles where wind direction is variable (Fig. 12.2a) between stakes 4–5 metres apart.
- take care not to twist the tape (Fig. 12.2c) between stakes. The 'hum' is produced when the wind hits the tape's flat side and it must be tied so that the 'flat' always flips back into the wind. A taut stretch ensures that this happens.
- to protect areas of a half hectare or more, place the lines at intervals of 10 to 20 metres. Users must experiment to achieve the best results.
- when judging how high to fix the tape remember that it must hang above the fully grown crop.

Reduce the bird colony wherever possible, to a level where it no longer poses a threat to yields. Collective effort is essential. Every egg of the pest species picked off, every nest knocked down and every fledgling that is killed reduces the size of the flock.

Rodents

Mice and rats cause serious losses both in the field and to stored grain. These animals are hunted by snakes but as land is cleared, ploughed up or built on, living sites for snakes decrease and so rodent populations increase. They can be poisoned or trapped. To poison small herbivores (plant eaters) that are chewing your crop prepare the following bait:

100 g bran, bean flour or mealie meal
10 g sugar
The infusion of half a cigarette in a cup of water (Unit 8).
Mix all this to a crumbly dough and place it in a can whose ends have been cut off (Fig. 12.3). Site it near the damaged plants. Rats feed at night. Do not mix the bait with a hand, only with a stick or spoon. Do not let domestic animals into the field while the bait is there.
Wash your hands as soon as you have finished handling the bait.

Place it near where the damage has occurred, in a tin that has had its ends cut off (Fig. 12.3). When it can be seen that the damage has stopped remove the container.

Baited foods to kill rodents are on the market under various trade names Coumatetralyle, Warfarin, etc. The manufacturer's instructions for use are printed on the packets and should be followed carefully. These compounds are fatal to warm-blooded creatures and should on no account be left within the reach of children.

The simplest traps to prepare are the pitfall types (Fig. 12.4), which can be adapted to catch mice or slugs.

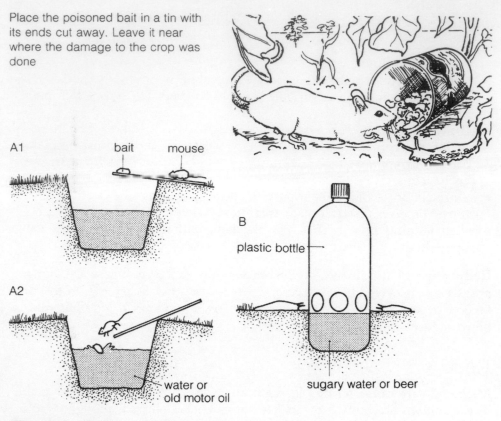

Place the poisoned bait in a tin with its ends cut away. Leave it near where the damage to the crop was done

A1   bait   mouse

A2
water or
old motor oil

B
plastic bottle

sugary water or beer

Fig. 12.3 Bait in a field container (Top right)
Fig. 12.4 Pitfall traps (Lower left)

Summary of unit 12   Nematodes, snails, birds and rodents

1. Nematodes (sometimes called eel worms) can attack roots. They travel very slowly but infected plants must be removed. If this is not possible, and the worms are always in the soil, an appropriate rotation will keep their numbers down.
2. Snails and slugs are a problem only during the rains or in swampy areas. They threaten young shoots or seedlings but are not otherwise important.
3. Birds can be kept from ripening grain by bending the seed-heads over. They can be kept off seed-beds and low growing crops by an arrangement of humming tapes. The tapes are most effective in a gusting wind.
4. Poisoned baits and traps should be set for small mammals, but poisons must be removed from the field as soon as the animal has been killed.
5. Pitfall traps avoid the use of poison bait.

DISEASES

UNIT 13   Plant parasites

Fungi

The fungi that most people are familiar with are mushrooms – some edible, some poisonous – which spring up in the rainy season. These strange parasitic plants are never green, have no leaves or flowers, and in place of roots have a mass of white threads.

A few fungi grow on tree trunks. Most appear to be growing in the soil but are, in fact growing on plant remains in the soil. Not being green, fungi cannot photosynthesise so they depend on the food developed by other plants.

An exception is *Striga*, the witchweed, a semi-parasitic plant with green leaves and pink or red flowers. This odd herb flowers, ripens seed and photosynthesises like any other weed but only germinates near certain grasses. These produce the chemical without which it cannot get started. It is a serious parasite on sorghum and millet.

Many fungi that grow on leaves, fruits and stems are so small that they are invisible without a microscope. Farmers see only the diseases they cause, or sometimes a powdery mat that covers the diseased parts and which is composed of the spores that serve the fungus as seed (Fig. 13.1c). Fungal disease is not easy to identify. The signs – yellowing, wilting, withering – are similar to those produced by frost, poor nutrition, nematodes, bacteria or other factors.

Most microscopic fungi are saprophytes, breaking up dead plant parts and returning them to the soil. Others are parasites, feeding on living plants and in the process causing wilts and other diseases. Many are parasites at one stage of their life cycle and saprophytes at another. Fungi that parasitise crops put farmers' livelihoods at risk for once the fungus has appeared in a crop it is too late to effect a cure. Fungi must be controlled before the

a

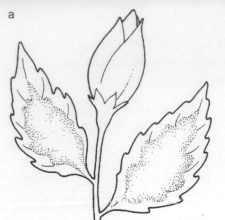

A leaf, to the eye covered in a whitish dust is in fact covered with a mass of microscopic feeding and fruiting cells.

b

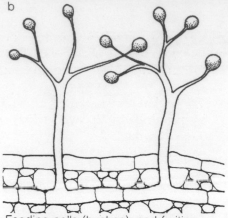

Feeding cells (hyphae), and fruiting bodies (sporangia), magnified about 900 times, growing on a leaf surface.

c

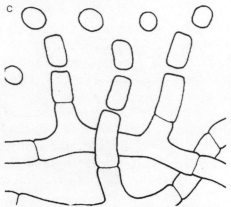

When ripe, the fruiting bodies release spores which drift in the air or fall to the ground from where they can be splashed onto new hosts by raindrops.

d

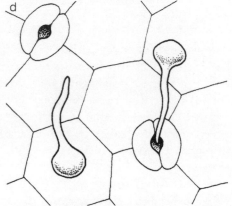

Once on a suitable host they germinate and enter the host cells through a pore or wound. The germinating spore can dissolve cell walls. Magnified 900 times.

e

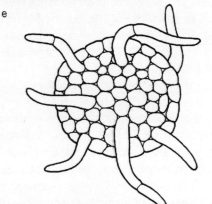

If weather conditions become too dry or cold for growth the fungus will develop a resting stage – which will settle on debris or in the soil.

f

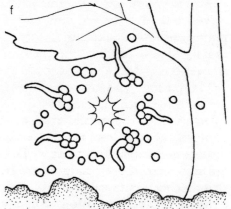

When conditions improve this resting stage bursts, releasing spores. These are carried by air or water to infect nearby host plants

Fig. 13.1 Life cycle of the downy mildew (*Peronospora*) Not to scale

disease is seen and the farmer does not know whether they are present in the field or not. It is always safest to assume that they are present.

Parasitic fungi can be roughly divided into:

- Those that attack plants above ground level and which can be controlled by prophylactic (preventative) spraying or by cultural methods.
- Those that attack through the root system, and cannot be controlled by sprays but only by rotation or cultural methods that ensure a dry micro-climate. Fungicides sold as 'soil drenches' to protect root systems are useful only where the amount of soil to be treated is small, for example in nursery beds.

A fungus often confines its attack to one plant family (see Unit 14 for a list of plant families). For example melon, gourd and pumpkin are all threatened by the powdery mildew; onions and cereals are not. But other fungi are more generally adapted and will attack not only living plants from a number of plant families but can live saprophytically as well as parasitically.

The life cycles of plant parasitic fungi (Fig. 13.1), like those of insects, are divided into growth stages and rest stages. In the growth stage spores are produced (Fig. 13.1c) that are spread by wind, rain-splash or insects. When the spores land on a suitable host they grow by means of tiny thread-like cells which enter the plant through leaf-pores (Fig. 13.1d), or through wounds made by insects, or accidents. They grow to produce spores which under suitable conditions produce further generations. The fungus can also develop a resting stage (Fig. 13.1e) which lies in the soil until conditions are right for germination.

Spores can spread in a number of ways. Those carried by wind can travel enormous distances. Rusts originating in Mexico have been known to infect wheat 3000 kilometres away in Canada, but spores dispersed by rain do not travel more than a few centimetres. Spores carried by insects usually infect plants in the immediate area. This becomes important when controls are being planned.

Bacteria and their control

Bacteria are smaller and simpler than fungi and can never be seen without a microscope. Most live on dead plant materials but a few parasitise living plants and cause brown or black rots. When they destroy roots or block a plant's water conducting tubes the plant wilts and dies. They do not form spores but some can survive for a long time by surrounding themselves with a protective coating which prevents them from drying out.

They grow in wet conditions and disperse in water films and by rain splash. Some species are transmitted from plant to plant by insects. Others adhere to seeds. Planting material such as sugar cane stems or root sections of banana are at risk because these must stay moist till planted.

Bacteria can be suppressed in the following ways:

- Dipping cuttings in a 0.5% solution of disinfectant before planting them into the field.
- Use of crop rotation. The following example, of a rotation designed to keep bacterial blight of potatoes from building up to pest proportions, will control the population growth of many other pathogens.

1st season: potatoes are grown.	The bacteria multiply and when the crop is lifted go into resting stage.
2nd season: beans are grown.	The bacteria cannot live on this crop. Many die but some remain in a resting stage.
3rd season: maize is grown.	This too does not nourish the bacteria and they are further reduced.
4th season: grow okra, onions or cabbage-type crops.	The pest population is cut to very small numbers. It will be safe to plant potatoes or other Solenaceae next season.

- Bacteria cannot survive dry conditions for long. Where bacterial wilt is a risk, the soil is ploughed and then left for a good part of the dry season to dry out before the next crop is put in. This is known as bare fallowing and is especially necessary when bush has just been cleared for crops. There are no effective sprays.

Viruses and their control

Viruses are smaller than bacteria and can be seen only with a powerful electron microscope. They exist in living cells. Virus diseases may take a long time to recognise as often the only effect on the crop is a gradual loss of vigour. Plants are small and yields drop or cease. Sometimes the signs of infection are obvious; red or yellow streaks appear on grasses and blotchy 'mosaic' markings on the leaves of other plants, but it is often difficult to tell viral disease from mineral deficiency. Growers should keep their local extension agents informed.

Viruses are spread when infected stem, tuber or root sections are planted. They multiply in the new plants. Sucking insects (such as aphids) can transfer viruses from plant to plant. Nematodes can carry them between roots. Some viruses can survive drying and heat. The tobacco mosaic virus, which infects tomato as well as tobacco, is transmitted in cigarette smoke.

Viruses are suppressed by:

- Controlling nematodes and aphids.
- Using virus free planting material.
- Spacing plants so that they do not touch.
- Not smoking in the field
- Removing and burning infected plants the moment they are found.

There are no effective sprays.

Mineral deficiency

If a plant is not supplied with sufficient amounts of the elements it needs for good growth it will develop symptoms of that lack of nourishment. These symptoms can be brittle or hollow stems, thin or pale leaves, yellow or red mottling on the leaves, distortions, die-back of shoots or root tips and leaf scorching. Growth will be poor and fruit and flowers may never develop. Deficiencies develop most readily on light sandy soils that let rain water through easily and allow nutrients to leach away.

With annual crops the element in short supply may be added in time to save the harvest but if trees have been planted on too sandy a soil years of work are wasted. Fertilising the orchard may be so expensive as to make the work pointless, and may in any case be ineffective. Always check the sites of proposed tree plantings, particularly of citrus, with an extension officer specialising in tree fruit crops.

Striga The witchweed and its control

This curious plant, with attractive pink or red flowers, can destroy a crop of sorghum. The minute seeds of *Striga* are produced in enormous numbers and can remain alive in the soil for years, particularly in dry conditions. They are stimulated to germinate by a substance from the host root which must not be more than 1 cm away. The parasite stays underground for 3–6 weeks, then emerges, its leaves turn green and start to photosynthesise. They depend on the host plant for water and minerals. The appearance of a few plants indicates a widespread problem underground for only a few of the parasites come up and produce seed. If the infestation is not dealt with it can make sorghum cultivation impossible in years to come. A serious infestation resembles drought. The crop wilts and turns yellow, remains stunted and dies.

Control is by rotation as follows:

- The seeds are stimulated by roots of cowpea, cotton, sunflower, sesame, sunhemp and groundnut but cannot parasitise these crops. Include them in rotations to rid the land of the parasite.
- A 'trap crop' of Sudan grass or susceptible sorghum is thickly sown and ploughed in after two months growth. The *Striga* germinates in large numbers, then dies when its host is killed. This method is extremely effective and at the same time fertilizes the ground. The parasite seems to avoid highly fertile land.

UNIT 14 Integrated disease management

The cultural practises described in Unit 5 for the control of insects also help to keep at bay outbreaks of fungal disease. An important difference is that sprays and dusts cannot cure fungal diseases. Once fungus has appeared in a field all that any treatment can do is slow its progress and this may not save the crop.

Successful spraying against fungi is, therefore, preventative – carried out before any disease is seen. The time to start spraying may be dictated by the weather – for instance when the soil warms after the cold season, or by the plant – for instance just before flowers form. The experience of past seasons is the farmer's guide.

The cultural practises that limit fungal diseases are familiar; many are as old as agriculture. Scientists studying the environment are now uncovering the reasons why these methods succeed. They have established some of the ways in which natural forces act to limit micro-organisms, just as they do insects. Some of their findings are listed here.

Cultural practices that limit disease

1. Genetic resistance of crops to fungi is so useful that every major seed company sells specially bred resistant seed. Planting resistant varieties can save growers much trouble. Unfortunately such resistances, developed in temperate climates, may be altered by the high temperatures and other conditions of the tropics. In the end local crop varieties, which have adapted to the local diseases, may do better than introduced varieties. The advice of extension staff should be sought and the experience of local farmers be noted.

2. Weeding, cultivation, pruning, ridging and spacing all help to create air movement and a drier micro-climate (the temperature and humidity of the air immediately under the crop). Spores, like other life forms, need moisture so the lack of it prevents them from germinating. The same practises separate individual plants creating gaps that spores cannot cross, particularly spores dispersed by rain splash. During growth this separation disappears but the crop will have been protected while small and tender.

Nursery beds should never be overcrowded. Fungi are, of necessity, always present in rich, well balanced soil, but in well airated, relatively dry *beds they are* less likely to establish themselves on the seedlings.

75

3. Crop hygiene practices   These include the following:

- Removal of debris from the crop previously in the field. This clears fields of parasitic spores that have gone into a resting stage.
- Removal of plant debris while the crop is growing. This clears the field of diseased leaves and fruits that would otherwise be centres from which infection could spread.
- Removal of infected plants. Burn or hot-compost these (Fig. 14.1). Heat kills the spores.
- Choosing clean seed. Growers that save their own seeds must be sure they come from healthy, disease-free plants and that the seed has been kept in dry, insect-free storage. To be sure your seed is clean, before planting, place it in a bag with a spoonful of fungicidal powder and shake it. Seed supplied commercially is often already so treated. On no account should this seed be eaten or stored near food grains.

4. Crop rotation   deprives spores of suitable hosts. The life cycle cannot continue and the spores are starved. Most fungi will not parasitise more than one family. A good rotation alternates between the plant families below.

Solenaceae:	Tomato, potato, peppers, eggplant, the rough eggplant djakatou, tobacco.
Cucurbitaceae:	Cucumber, bitter cucumber, melon, water-melon, pumpkin, courgette, gourd.
Leguminosae:	Peas, beans, bamabara groundnut, groundnut.
Malvaceae:	Okra, kenaf, roselle, cotton.
Cruciferae:	Cabbages, cauliflower, broccoli, radish, beet, turnip.
Lilaceae:	Onions, garlic, shallot, leek.
Graminacae:	Maize, sorghum, millet, sugarcane, wheat, rice.
Compositae:	Lettuce, sunflower, pyrethrum.
Convulvulaceae:	Sweet potato

Plants within a family should not succeed each other in the same bed. Each crop should be separated by two seasons in which crops from other families are grown.

5. Intercropping   separates crops by space as rotation separates them by time. The crops used must come from different family groups. Intercropping is particularly effective against spores spread by rain splash.

6. Manuring   with crops specially grown for this purpose and ploughed in when tender (green manuring) adds fertility to the soil and produces healthy plants which resist fungal attack. Manuring with fresh dung, or mixtures that include fresh dung, does the same but in addition suppresses fungi. Why this is so is not yet clear but there is evidence that plants manured in this way produce protective compounds. Fig. 14.1 describes how to make sprays based on a compost of fresh dung plus other ingredients.

76

7. Planting dates can sometimes be adjusted to avoid seasons of high risk.

Chemical controls

Minerals kill fungi, and sulphur and lime are ingredients of several popular fungicides. Metallic salts such as copper sulphate have been used for over a century and sodium bicarbonate is proving increasingly useful. Recent research has found that dung and urine also have fungicidal action.

Fungicides can be roughly divided into:

- those used as foliar (leaf) sprays against mildews (fungi which produce a white or grey growth on plant surfaces),
- those used as foliar sprays against other fungi,
- those used as soil drenches (poured into the earth),
- those used as seed dressing dusts.

When to spray If growers knew which disease was likely to appear in any particular season, they could spray just before the time of its appearance. Most of the time they do not know exactly and so must spray soon after the crop at risk has started growing and long before the appearance of disease. This is called prophylactic spraying.

What sprays to use For the same reason – not knowing what might attack crops – growers use mixtures designed to kill a wide range of disease fungi. The exceptions are the Cucurbit crops such as melon and cucumber which are susceptible to mildews. In this case sulphur or sodium bicarbonate are the correct sprays. Some natural fungicides are described in this section. A few are also village-available.

To give good protection fungicides must cover a plant completely. Spores are in the air all the time, and will inevitably land on the crop, and only a complete covering of fungicide will stop them establishing themselves. Both the upper and lower leaf surfaces must be sprayed. Take special care to cover leaves near the ground because these are the ones most at risk from spores splashed up onto them by rain drops.

How often to spray depends very much on how dangerous, to the crop's health or the grower's income, a disease is likely to be. Most fungicides have a low persistence in the tropics and must be applied weekly. Crops must be sprayed promptly after rain showers or over-head irrigation.

Fungicidal sprays

1. Bordeaux mixture (Similar to Burgandy Mixture and Cheshant Mixture.) Use of a foliar spray against all fungi except mildews.
Formulation: soluble powder.
Doseage: 25 g in a litre of water.

To prepare 10 litres of Bordeaux Mixture:

- dissolve 150 g of copper sulphate in 2 litres of water,
- dissolve 100 g of lime in 2 litres of water,
- mix the two solutions thoroughly and add 6 litres of water,
- stir in a handful of soap and filter the mixture through a cloth or through the basket filter of your spray tank.

Interval before harvest Crops are safe to eat three days after spraying

2. Sulphur A naturally occurring, yellow rock, sold as a powder in agricultural supply shops or by chemists.

Use as a dust over leaves or, mixed with a handful of soap, as a foliar spray against mildews.

Formulation: A fine powder. If it is sold as rocky lumps it should be crushed to a smooth powder by pounding it in a mortar or placing it in a cloth bag and rolling a bottle back and forth across it.

Doseage: 0.5% suspension – 5 g in a litre.

To prepare 10 litres:

- measure 50 g (6 rounded teaspoons or half a tea-glass) of powder,
- mix into 1 litre (10 teaglasses) of cold clean water,
- add a handful of soap and stir so that the powder is well dispersed, and suspended throughout the water,
- fill your spray tank quarter full of water,
- filter in the suspension; then top up to half tank level.

Application: While spraying shake the tank every few minutes to keep the powder dispersed in the water.

Interval before harvest: Crops are safe to eat two days after spraying.

3. Sodium bicarbonate   (Bicarbonate of Soda, baking powder and anti-acid tablets under various trade names.)

Uses: As a spray to control blue rots on stored oranges, as a foliar spray for powdery mildews on pepper, cucumber and gooseberry plants. It appears to be a useful, all purpose fungicide (Fig 14.2)

Formulation: White powder or tablets, readily soluble, found in general stores and chemists shops.

Doseage: 1.0% solution – 10 g in a litre.

To prepare 10 litres:

- dissolve 100 g sodium bicarbonate in a litre of cold clean water,
- stir in a handful of soap,
- filter through a cloth or the basket filter of your sprayer,
- add 9 litres of cold clean water or, if using a knapsack sprayer, half fill it with water. (A knapsack sprayer holds about 20 litres.)

If signs of disease have appeared a solution of twice the strength might halt an attack. It can harm leaves, so try it on one plant before spraying the crop. It is safe to use with twig-bunches as described in Unit 6. Figure 14.2 shows the sort of teaglass used for these recommendations and also shows what a rounded heap of powder on a spoon looks like. Measure the correct amount with 'kitchen' equipment.

Interval before harvest: None. Sodium bicarbonate is safe to take but wash food to get rid of the sour taste of the chemical. In the field it persists for a long time.

4. Watery compost extract   Recent research has shown that fermented water infusions of compost made partly from fresh animal manure give effective protection against fungi. The compost itself has no fungicidal action but seems to stimulate leaves to produce fungus-resistant chemicals of their own. To prepare WCE see Fig. 14.1 and below.

- Prepare compost by piling together plant remains, fresh animal dung and other organic wastes. At least some of the plant remains must be fresh and moist. Any dry plant remains should be chopped up small for easier rotting. The pile as a whole must be moist but not soggy. Air as well as moisture are necessary for the material to rot.
- Cover the pile and leave it for two to three weeks. It must heat up to 70° C at the centre and after two or three days this can be tested by thrusting a stick into the centre for a few minutes, withdrawing it and feeling its end. It should be hot to the touch.
- When the heat has died down the compost is ready and the infusion can be prepared at any time after this.
- To make an infusion that does not injure the crop, mix at the rate of one spadeful of compost to a pail of water. Leave this for two weeks
- Filter the extract, which will be a rich brown colour, into your sprayer, stir in a handful of soap. The solid material remaining after the extract has been used makes good fertiliser. Dig it into the soil.

5. Neem and garlic are said to have fungicidal action when infused and sprayed as described in Unit 9.

Table 14.1   Synthetic fungicides

---

1. Thiram   Trade names: Arasan, Therasan, etc.
- **Use** as soil and seed fungicide and as a foliar spray.
- **Formulation**: Powder.
- **Doseage**: 20–25 g in 10 l of water.
- **Interval before harvest**: 15 days.
- **Caution**: Can leave a bad taste on produce; can cause skin irritation.

---

2. Zineb   Trade names: Dithane Z–78, Polyram, etc.
- **Use** as spray on leaves and fruits.
- **Formulation**: Powder.
- **Doseage**: 20–25 g in 10 l of water.
- **Interval before harvest**: 15–30 days.
- **Caution**: Can irritate skin, nose and eyes.

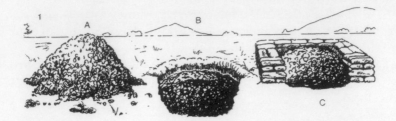

1. Compost is made of all kinds of waste – moist plant-remains, dry plant-remains cut small, household waste, dung and soil, but it must include some fresh animal dung. It can be piled up (A), put in a pit (B), or in an enclosure (C). Make it in 1–2 days.

2. Cover with heavy sacking for 2–3 weeks. The bacteria that break up wastes need warm dark, moist conditions.

3. To test if it is rotting well, push a stick into the centre of the pile. Leave it for a few minutes. When taken out the end of the stick should be hot to the touch.

4. To test its readiness sow some seeds on the pile. If they germinate the compost can now be used to make the water extract.

5. Into a container throw a spadeful of compost and add a pail of water. This makes roughly a 1 : 6 dilution

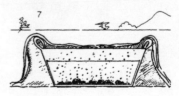

6. Cover the container and leave it to ferment for 6–8 days. During this time the extract forms. It will be a rich, dark brown colour.

7. Filter the liquid into your sprayer. Do not dilute, but as usual add a handful of soap to help 'spread' the spray.

Fig. 14.1 How to make watery compost extract

3. Captan   Trade names: Orthocide, etc.
- **Use** as spray, or seed and soil fungicide.
- **Formulation**: Powder.
- **Doseage**: 10 g of powder in 10 l of water.
- **Interval before harvest:** 15 days.
- **Caution**: May cause skin irritation. Can poison fish.

4. Dinocap   Trade names: Karathane, etc.
- **Use** as spray against powdery mildews.
- **Formulation**: Powder.
- **Doseage**: 10 g powder in 10 l of water.
- **Interval before harvest**: 2 days.
- **Caution**: Do not use in very hot weather.

5. Maneb   Trade names: Manage, Dithane M–22, etc.
- **Use** as leaf spray particularly against cercospora and anthracnose.
- **Formulation**: Powder.
- **Doseage**: 20–25 g in 10 l.
- **Interval before harvest**: 15–30 days.
- **Caution**: Can be irritating to skin, eyes and nose.

There are no synthetic sprays against bacteria or viruses. There is some evidence that an infusion of garlic applied as a spray gives protection.

Creating a database – The pesticide record

Crops new in an area will grow free of problems for a time but eventually diseases will appear and might destroy crops over a wide region. Extension staff might be able to identify the cause but often have to send plant samples to a laboratory for identification and advice. This is important for the future cultivation of that crop.

It is only in the past century that agricultural research has become the work of scientists. Before that research was carried out by farmers. Most major crop improvements, for example the selection of cereals from the wild originals to the types grown today, was complete before the Pharaohs ceased to rule Egypt.

Our research is still farmer-led. Information from growers builds a picture of the diseases that threaten crops in a region. Researchers depend on this field knowledge to guide them to the problems they should be looking into. This is why it is important to keep a record of sprays used during the growing season.

1. Date: _____ Crop: _____ Village: _____

2. Description of damage: _____

3. Extent of damage: Half of field. _____ Over half of field. _____ Other _____

4. Distribution of damage: _____ Isolated plants. _____ Blocks _____

5. Type of irrigation: Flooded basin. _____ Flooded furrow. _____
   Hand watering. _____ Sprinklers. _____ None.

7. Weather conditions: Temperature. _____ Cloud cover. _____
   Relative humidity, _____ Wind _____

8. Soil moisture: Damp. _____ Dry. _____

9. Soil temperature: At finger-nail depth. _____ At finger depth. _____

10. Fungicide used and date
    1.
    2.

11. Was the harvest good, _____ fair, _____ or poor. _____

This sheet is a guide and it is not supposed that every question will be answered and every item completed. What the damage looked like (2), how it was spread (3, 4), what sprays were used to treat the crop (10) and with what result (11) is the information on which the database is built.

Everyone can develop his or her own 'kitchen measures' for pesticides. Remember to store the mixing bowls with the tank and chemicals well out of the way of children and cooking pots.

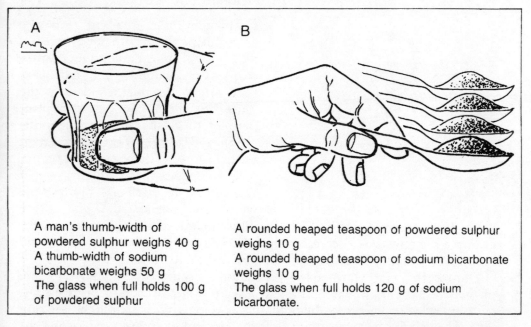

A

B

A man's thumb-width of powdered sulphur weighs 40 g
A thumb-width of sodium bicarbonate weighs 50 g
The glass when full holds 100 g of powdered sulphur

A rounded heaped teaspoon of powdered sulphur weighs 10 g
A rounded heaped teaspoon of sodium bicarbonate weighs 10 g
The glass when full holds 120 g of sodium bicarbonate.

Fig. 14.2 Kitchen measures for field use

84

Summary of units 13 to 14   Plant parasites, diseases, fungicides and IPM

1. Microscopic plant parasites include fungi and the even smaller bacteria and viruses.

2. Fungi, whether large or microscopic, cannot photosynthesise and depend on plants for their food.

3. Most fungi are saprophytes, some are parasites. Some include both states in their life cycles.

4. Only preventative action such as rotation or prophylactic spraying can protect crops against fungi.

5. To protect Cucurbits against mildew spray sulphur or sodium bicarbonate. A watery compost extract also gives good protection.

6. Against other fungi use copper sulphate/lime sprays (Bordeaux and similar mixtures), or Watery Compost Extract or sodium bicarbonate.

7. Against bacteria and viruses there are no sprays. Careful husbandry is the only precaution.

8. Record your own experiences in order to build a database and help local growers to raise their yields and plan their farm operations with better security than previously.

9. Rotation systems keep the pest population in your soil down. The procedure is as follows. In any one field:

   a) Grow the susceptible crop (the crop at risk from disease).
   b) Follow it with an unrelated crop.
   c) Follow this with a crop unrelated to the first two.
   d) Follow this with a crop unrelated to the first three.
   e) You may now safely plant the susceptible crop again.

10. Plants are arranged in families of near-related varieties. These plant families are usually attacked by the same pests and diseases so that separating them in time (by rotation) controls the pests and diseases.

PROTECTING CROPS FROM
LARGER ANIMALS AND WIND

UNIT 15 Keeping animals out of the garden

Traditionally, in semi-arid (low rainfall) regions, farmers have used branches torn from thorn trees to protect their gardens against grazing animals. Ominously, in many places this barrier material is becoming hard to find as rising populations consume firewood and fencing faster than the trees can replace themselves.

The loss of trees has important consequences for the soil, for temperatures and for the growth of other vegetation. Tree roots help to hold soil in place. Also, evapo-transpiration (the process by which trees draw moisture from the ground and pass it into the atmosphere) cools the ground and the air (Fig. 15.1). Hence governments with semi-arid areas within their borders are now increasingly passing tree protection laws that make it illegal to collect thorn fence. A practical, permanent solution to this problem is to grow live fencing, i.e. hedges. Wire fencing is prohibitively expensive and has no uses besides security. Growers who put in hedges will have, for an investment of time rather than money, security plus valuable additional crops at the borders of their gardens.

The ideal hedge

A good hedge should:

- be thorny,
- grow branches to replace any chopped off; a process known as coppicing,
- be strong and a quick grower, with woody stems,
- produce a marketable product,
- discourage grazing animals.

No one plant satisfies all these conditions, so farmers compromise. They plant multiple rows, add ditches or banks to make the boundaries more impenetrable and mix varieties. The hedges can yield fodder, fruit and medicines. Depending on the climate, the plants chosen and the care taken to establish and nurture it, a hedge will mature in 2–5 years from planting. It may be started in any of three ways:

- by direct seeding,
- by transplanting seedlings or previously rooted cuttings,
- by direct planting of large cuttings – the method described in this unit.

Table 15.1 illustrates and describes some of the plants that grow readily and so are useful in establishing hedges. The list is far from complete. Agents who want to see local resources being used to the full could, at the start of the rains, help farmers plant cuttings from various of the region's plants and a year later collect the information as to their success. A village or cooperative group that pools its efforts can become immensely knowledgeable in a relatively short time.

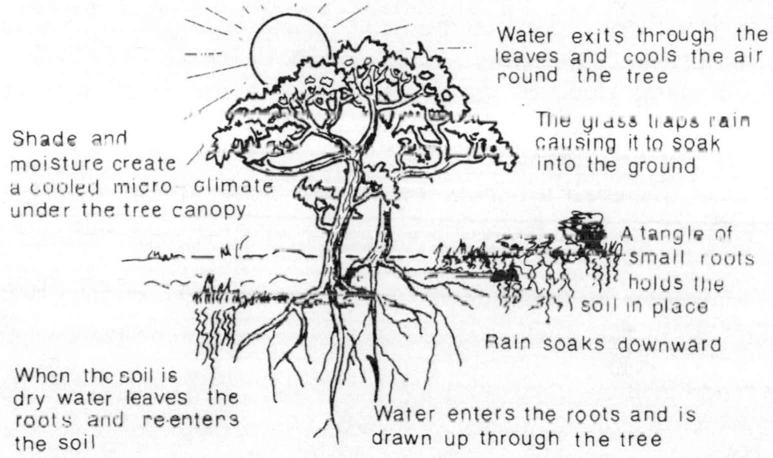

Plants, whether they are cabbages or trees, create their own microclimate. This is a layer of temperature and humidity different from that further from the plant. The air inside the leaf crown of a date palm, for instance, can be 10 degrees cooler than the air outside the palm. This difference is caused by evapotranspiration, the process that draws water up from the roots and out through the leaves, and also by shading. The first cools the plant and the air about it, the second cools the ground underneath it. In this way plants change local climatic conditions.

Fig. 15.1 Evapotranspiration and microclimate

The manner of starting depends on the plant, Some need considerably less care than others.

- 'Direct seed' means these seeds germinate quickly with very few failures.
- 'Seed in pots' means 25–60% of seeds are likely to germinate. The proportion may be raised by pre-treating the seeds (see below), but to avoid gaps growers should grow the seedlings in pots and then transplant rather than simply rely on direct seeding.
- 'Stem cuttings' means large cuttings will take root within one season.
- 'Root cuttings' are large sections cut from roots just as sections are cut from stems.
  Some seeds when planted fresh from the tree germinate quickly, whereas if dried and stored they need some treatment.

Seed pre-treatments are ways of ensuring water gets past the harder outer husk of the seeds and penetrates quickly into the growing part, the seed germ. Thus the seeds will germinate right away. There are two methods. You might have to test a few seeds to discover which method is best for a particular plant.

- Soak the seeds in water overnight before planting. Sometimes the water must be hot.
- Clip, cut, file or otherwise injure the hard seed coat just before planting.

Growth often depends on rainfall. Trees growing at the lower end of their water requirement may never grow over bush size (1–3 m high). In wetter conditions they may become trees. A bush, which together with its neighbours forms a thorny thicket, will be more use as a hedge than trees would be.

Table 15.1 Hedging plants

Species	Least water needed	Bee food	Cattle Fodder	Growth habit	Manner of starting	Other uses
1. *Euphorbia balsamifera*	150 mm/yr	No	No	Thicket	Stem cuttings	None known
2. *Euphorbia tirucalli*	350 mm/yr	No	No	Thicket	Stem cuttings	None known
3. *Commiphora africana*	150 mm/yr	Yes	Yes	Thorn tree	Stem cuttings	Medicinal gum
4. *Accasia macrostachya*	500 mm/yr	No	Yes	Thorn tree	Seed in pots	Edible fruit
5. *Agave sisilana*	500 mm/yr	No	Yes	Thorn bush	Root cuttings	Fibre
6. *Ziziphus mauritiana*	150 mm/yr	Yes	Yes	Thorn tree	Seed in pots	Medicine
7. *Prosopis juliflora*	200 mm/yr	Yes	Yes	Tree	Direct seeding	None known
8. *Parkinsonia aculeata*	400 mm/yr	Yes	No	Thorn tree	Direct seeding	Edible shoots
9. *Accasia ataxacantha*	500 mm/yr	Yes	Yes	Thorn tree	Seed in pots	None known

Start the hedge at the beginning of the rains. This might conflict with the planting of crops but will save work later. Hedges, like any plants that stay green throughout the dry season, must not, save in their first few weeks, be irrigated. They survive best when they are forced to push their roots down into the water table.

The water table

Four things can happen to rain that falls on land:

- It flows to lower areas and ends up in the sea or in lakes.
- It is sucked up by vegetation and evaporates through leaves into the air (a process called evapo-transpiration).
- It lies on the surface and evaporates directly into the air.
- It seeps into the ground and is either used immediately by shallow rooted plants or sinks deep and is stored as underground water.

This underground store is replenished by rain. Its level (the water table), rises and falls depending on how much is fed in by rainfall and how much is taken out through wells or by crops and other vegetation. Wells must reach into the water table in order to stay filled; plants must root into the wetted but still aerated layer just above it (the phreatic or root zone) in order to survive without irrigation. After the rains the water table is at its highest level; just before the rains it is at its lowest level. Good hedge plants have roots that follow the retreating root zone and adapt quickly to its changes. At these deepest levels they do not take the soil-water used by shallower rooted crops.

Cuttings

The quickest way to establish a hedge is to plant sections of stem (called cuttings) taken from plants with this deep rooting characteristic. Many trees and shrubs will grow from cuttings but only a few species root quickly enough to establish themselves within the months of a short, and perhaps unreliable, rainy season. Hedges must be established quickly and planting cuttings directly where needed is, for the following reasons, the best way to do this.

- Cuttings cost little or no money.
- The method uses local plants whose growth patterns are familiar to the farmers of the region.
- Cuttings are easy to see, protect and weed during establishment.
- They are well adapted to local rainfall, pests and diseases.
- They will be exactly the same as the parent plant.
- Unlike seeds they are always available at planting time.
- They grow quickly. Planted at the start of the rains they will be securely rooted by the middle of the season.

1. The start of the rains is the right time.

2. Choose healthy plants.

3. Cut older stems; 2–4 cm in diameter.

4. Mark the top end with a notch or a piece of string.

5. Keep the cuttings cool and damp. Shade and cover them.

6. Move them to the planting site fast, within 12 hours.

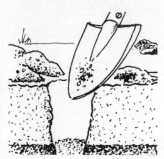

7. Dig the planting hole down to damp soil or sand

8. Half-fill the hole with water and while it drains . . .

9. re-cut the base of the cutting on a slant.

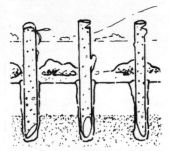

10. Plant the sticks 30 cm deep and 30 cm apart

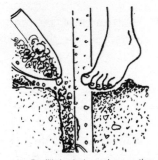

11. Re-fill the hole and press the soil or sand down firmly . . .

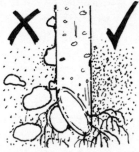

12. so that no air gaps are left in the root zone.

Fig. 15.2 Establishing a hedge with cuttings. Here *Euphorbia balsamifera* is being used.

The time to plant is at the start of the rains, and if the rains are late or poor, the cuttings must be irrigated. Do this generously because only in soil deeply soaked will the cuttings develop the long roots that reach the water, and enable the hedge to survive dry seasons and poor rains. Date palms suckers (shoots used as cuttings) are sometimes planted in pits dug a metre or more deep, at the bottom of which the soil is moist. This planting into the phreatic zone, assures good root development.

A good cutting must have at least four buds. It should be thick enough to contain a good store of plant food, woody enough so that it doesn't dry before the roots have had time to start, and young enough to have vigorous buds. Diameter is a good guide to choosing the right stems. They should be no thinner than a man's thumb (about 2 cm). The new roots will emerge from the growth cells near the buds.

For two years the cuttings will need to be guarded by thorns. Often they are started inside the old thorn barriers. In vegetable gardens they gain the advantage of treatments applied to the crops. They should be kept clean weeded and mulched if possible. It cannot be over emphasised that the hedge is a crop as important as any in the garden.

The form the hedge takes depends on what growers want. It can consist of double or triple rows. It can be placed on the flat or on a bank or behind a ditch.

A hedge is a permanent feature. If it has to be moved a great deal of labour will have been wasted so it must be carefully planned and all the farmers on whose land it borders should be consulted before it is put in.

UNIT 16   Strengthening the hedge

At the end of the first year a hedge will still need the protection of thorn branches because the young plants will not have grown entangled or woody enough to keep animals out of the crops. Large gaps between the plants must be plugged by layering. The young hedge can be supported and strengthened by bending and weaving.

LAYERING AND WEAVING

- Layering causes woody stems to produce roots while still attached to the parent plant. Plants which root from cuttings only after months in a mist house or irrigated nursery will root from a layered stem with relative ease. These rooted stems can then be cut from the parent stem and replanted where needed.
- Bending and weaving the young pliable branches creates a tangled lattice of stems that support each other and give the hedgerow strength and stability. It does not produce roots.

Layering

This is used on trees that are difficult to root. Mangoes are often layered into pots because their cuttings will hardly root, are very difficult to transplant successfully and if seeded do not always give the same fruit as the parent tree. Layering is best carried out at the start of the rains.

At certain, specialised points (called growth points or meristems) plant cells reproduce themselves. They do not simply enlarge, but increase in number and then enlarge. This causes the plant to grow longer and thicker. These growth cells have the power to develop as roots or shoots depending on where in the plant they are and whether they are above ground or below. Buds show the presence of a meristem – where new shoots or roots can be expected to develop. Thus, branches chosen for layering must, like those chosen for cuttings, be mature but not old and have well spaced, healthy buds. They should be at least one centimetre in diameter.

Plants vary a great deal in their response to layering. Among the trees which can be successfully layered from shoots are cinnamon, guava, acacia, and some species of citrus. *Tamarindus indica* a leguminous tree which has edible pulp and prefers semi-arid conditions, will also layer.

(a) Scrape the bark from a budding stem and cut off any leaves near the wound.

(b) Peg the injured part to the ground and tie the leafy tip of the stem to a stake so it is upright.

(c) Mound earth over the pegged section. Keep it moist for the next few months. Mulch and shade it to make the task easier.

(d) Roots will grow near to the injured part. When they are well developed the leafy tip will also have grown large. The whole rooted stem is now ready to be cut off its 'parent' and replanted where needed.

Fig. 16.1 Layering 'on site'

Creeping plants such as mint will quickly root from every node (where a leaf joins the stem) that touches moist soil, but most woody stems need at least a few months in warm, moist soil to start rooting. They root more reliably if they are wounded or scraped before being buried. Wounds stimulate rooting.

To layer choose a low growing branch and bend it down. Where it touches the ground wound it by slitting upward (Fig. 16.1), or by scraping off a few centimetres of the soft live bark. Trim the leaves from the parts near the wound and peg the stem into the earth making sure that the end of the stem, with a few leaves on it, is tied upright to a stake (Fig. 16.1b). Bury the injured section under a mound of soil (Fig. 16.1c). The buried section must have at least one, or better still two buds (Fig. 16.1a).

Keep the mound of soil damp during the weeks following. Even in the rains some irrigation might be necessary. The soil will stay moist longer if the site is shaded or mulched (covered with dry leaves or dung). After a time – which can be weeks or months, roots will grow from the buried section. When the new root system is strongly developed (Fig. 16.1d), the stem can be cut off and replanted wherever needed. It can also be left in place to make the hedge denser or fill gaps.

Fill gaps by layering low branches all along the hedge row. In this case there is no need to cut and replant. Increase the width of your hedge by layering suitable stems all the way down the row (Fig. 16.2). If this is done in the dry season the layered branches must be kept cool and moist by irrigation, plus shading and mulching. It increases the work and decreases the chances of 100% success but it might be easier to find time then, rather than in the busy season.

Bending and weaving

This is a quick way to fill gaps and strengthen the whole hedge row. Bend the young pliable branches horizontally and weave them about neighbouring stems. If necessary tie them in position. The new shoots grow directly upward (Fig. 16.3d) and may in their turn be bent over and woven. This creates a leafy lattice, made denser year by year as the process is repeated. It works well with mulberry trees and other species whose branches are pliable. This is a task for the dry season.

Older woody branches that will not bend must be half-cut and bent over. Make a slanting cut halfway through the branch (Fig. 16.3a). Carefully bend the branch horizontally and tie it in place to prevent any movement or damage other than the cut already made (Fig. 16.3b). The buds on the cut branch will shoot up in the normal manner (Fig. 16.3d), since they are still receiving water and nourishment through the undamaged part of the stem. The process can be repeated year after year. If the bent branches are too short to reach the next stem tie them to stakes put in for the purpose (Fig. 16.3c).

Stem sections slit and buried

Layer low growing branches along the hedge wherever there are gaps; or use this method to add an additional row to a hedge or windbreak.

Fig. 16.2 Layering to fill gaps

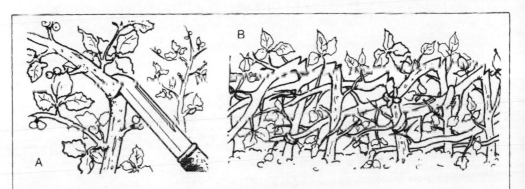

Slash branches halfway through on a slant (a). Bend them over to tie to nearby stems (b). Tying is preferable to weaving in order to fix slashed branches in position; weaving can cause further injuries at the cut. Pliable branches may be bent without first slashing. This gives a more 'open' type of hedge than slashing but bent branches may be woven in along the row and for some varieties may be the better method.

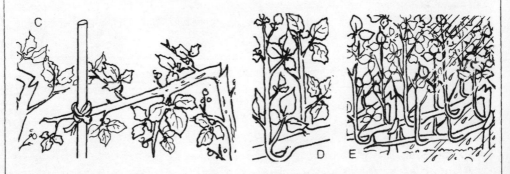

If a slashed branch is too short to reach the nearest stem, tie it to a stake put in for that purpose (c). The shoots develop vertically (d) growing across gaps (e). They can, in their turn, be woven or bent to increase the density of the hedge.

Fig. 16.3 Bending and interweaving

Recording local trees

Many species, other than those noted in Fig. 15.4, make useful barriers against wind or animals. When noting any trees that are being used in living fences, include the following points in your notes.

1. The date.
2. The village and district.
3. The local name of the plant.
4. The Latin name if known. (For botanical identification send a twig with leaves and a pod complete with seeds to the nearest botanist or university herbarium.)
5. The use to which the plant is being put; hedge, windbreak, shade, etc.
6. The length and height of the hedgerow.
7. The age of the hedgerow if known and the reasons for planting.
8. The manner of planting: direct seeding, cuttings, transplanting from pots, etc.
9. Problems of maintenance if any.
10. Will the owner agree to the agent trying out layering or coppicing on one of the hedge plants just to see what happens? There is a lack of this kind of information and research stations cannot fill all the gaps in our knowledge.

UNIT 17   Maintaining the hedge

When healthy plants are injured they put out new growth in place of that destroyed, new leaves in place of those grazed, roots in place of wounded bark. The loss of apical buds – at the tip of branches (Fig. 17.1a, b) is quickly compensated for by the growth of side shoots. The loss of side branches creates a stronger crown. Growers use these facts to thicken, re-shape and repeatedly harvest trees and bushes. By cutting

in a pre-planned manner shade trees are made to grow shadier and hedges denser. Yields of all sorts of products from fresh fodder to medicines, fruits and construction poles are increased.

Trimming   takes off the outer leaves and twigs and causes a fresh leafy layer to grow in their place. Trimming is most easily done with shears; it shapes the hedge. A good hedge is broader at the base than at the top. Light grazing can have the same effect as trimming. Carefully tethered livestock can do a grower's trimming for him if he takes care that they do not over-graze and shifts the stakes whenever necessary.

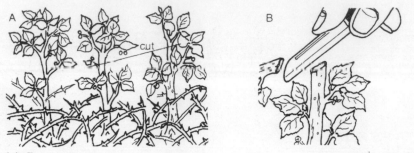

(a) For the first 2 years of growth the young hedge plants need the protection of thorn barriers. The saplings grow straight upward with very little meeting of side branches, so there are large gaps between the plants.

(b) With a sharp knife remove the apical buds shown here and in frame (a).

(c) With the removal of the apical bud the side shoots branch out and meet and entangle with each other. Gaps are covered and the hedge grows denser. Further trimming will keep it in shape and improve its cover.

Fig. 17.1 'Bushing out' the hedge

Pruning takes off more wood than trimming, and is selective. It removes branches that threaten to overbalance a tree, or that keep light from crops beneath it. It removes dead branches which might harbour parasites, fungi or insects. Cleaning a hedge in this way prevents the development of diseased shoots and consequently, gaps. It admits light which helps young shoots to develop. If it removes terminal buds then side-shoots will grow and the hedge will 'bush out' (Fig. 17.1c).

Lopping takes off entire branches which might be obstructing air movement or throwing too much shade. Lopping slows root growth and so lessens a tree's competition with crops for water. A lopped tree has a long, straight trunk and a heavy leaf crown.

Coppicing removes the main trunk of a tree to within 30 cm of the ground. It results in thicket – a close growing impenetrable woody barrier. It yields poles. Not all trees coppice, so ask at the regional tree nursery, and watch the trees in your area.

Pollarding removes the crown of a tree leaving the main trunk and stumps of branches. It creates a tree with a long trunk and a crown of slender, densely leafed branches. It also controls root growth.

All cuts must be cleanly made – cut all the way through, never tear branches off. Untidy wounds become infected, poison the tree and distort its growth or even slowly kill it. Appropriate tools are important.

UNIT 18 Protection from large animals

Gardens and fields on nomadic herding routes or where there are free range animals must have effective protection especially when the surrounding area is short of pasturage. Crops near national parks are at risk from animals often big enough to knock down or force their way through any fence. Therefore an effective deterrent will be composed of something the animal is unable or unwilling to cross.

Camels, for instance cannot negotiate any step that is greater than their knee height. The design of the ditch that keeps camels out of a garden must take this into account.

Dig a trench; mound the soil on the side nearest the garden so as to create a step 1.5m high (A). (A camel's leg is around 1.4m long). The side of the ditch furthest from the garden should have a gentle slope so that a camel can climb out easily (B); trapped animals lead to arguments with their owners. The hedge should be about a metre behind the mound, out of browsing reach. In some soils growers may have to reinforce the side of the trench in order to keep the steep profile (c).

Fig. 18.1 A ditch barrier against camels

Rough-ground barriers are effective against elephants. This method does not appear to have been tried against camels or donkeys. A fortunately placed agricultural agent or landowner could try this technique.

Spread rocks or shells in a shallow trench 2–3m wide – depending on the animal one is guarding against, and about 6cm deep (A). This prevents the rocks from being dispersed. The surface is uncomfortable to step on – too sharp or not steady enough, so the animal will not risk crossing it (B).

Fig. 18.2 A 'Rough-surface' strip

UNIT 19   Protection from wind

In windswept gardens crops grow slower, fruit later and stay smaller than in sheltered gardens. Even light winds dry leaf and soil surfaces and restrict growth. The damage done by strong winds can cut noticeably into a farmer's income. Wind can blow seed right out of sandy soils, making repeated sowing necessary. It can lift dry soil by the tonne and carry it elsewhere. It can spoil the appearance of crops by tearing delicate leaves or bat-

tering and scarring young fruits, making them unsaleable.

Yet when a windstorm is raging, the air at the centre of the forest, only 600 m across, can be almost still. Reducing the speed of wind starts a whole chain of beneficial climatic change. Evaporation slows, the soil retains moisture and soil temperature is lower. Plants transpiring the cooled soil-water lower the air temperature and increase relative humidity (the percent-age of water vapour in air). This lessens water stress on plants so that the vegetation grows faster and intercepts more rain. Sheltering a garden from wind protects crops from abrasion (injury from flying dust) and soil from erosion (removal). Livestock are shaded and less prone to heat exhaustion.

To achieve this growers and cooperatives with enough land and money can create shelter-belts (Fig. 19.1). On a smaller scale, the farmer who grows a hedge can design it as a windbreak

1. by letting the hedge grow tall,
2. by inter-planting it with taller trees (Fig. 19.2). This method gives a sturdier and longer-lasting structure than the first but takes longer to achieve.

Windbreaks

Windbreaks are rows of trees and shrubs planted in the path of prevailing winds. Even in places where winds are not strong, water is in good supply, and there seems no particular need for windbreaks, a hedge or shelterbelt can provide fuelwood, medicine, food for livestock, bees and people, mulch, and support for vine crops. There will also be some increase in growth due to lowered wind speeds.

Windbreaks work best at right angles to the wind (Fig. 19.1). Where the wind direction changes seasonally two or more boundaries may have to be designed as windbreak hedges. The design is important.

This provides cover at several separate levels (stories) above ground. Shrubs catch wind up to 2 m from ground level and exclude animals. Small trees shelter levels 2–5 m and larger trees from 5–10 m. Together they make an efficient wind filter whose effects can be felt 100 m or more from the trees.

Fig. 19.1 Multistorey windbreak

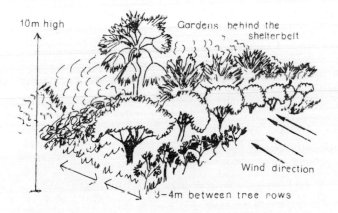

This will suit growers who have not enough land to put in a shelterbelt or who do not need anything as elaborate. If fruit trees are planted along the row their yields will be somewhat lower than if they were in a more sheltered position.

Fig. 19.2 Windbreak hedge interplanted with trees

How high must a windbreak be? The taller the hedge the greater the distance, measured at right angles to the hedgerow, that it shelters. Windspeed is reduced by as much as 60–70% over 3 to 5 tree-heights from the hedge. This means that a row of trees 10 m high protects up to 50 m of land. Further from the hedge windspeeds gradually recover and edge towards their original speed but reductions of 50% are usual up to 10 tree-heights from the hedge. Farmers will notice some improvement in yields as far as 100 m from a windbreak 10 m high.

Should the windbreak be solid? Good windbreaks filter and allow the passage of some wind. Without such safety gaps the hedge will take too much punishment and will not last well. Barriers without enough gaps create strong currents and eddies which batter the crop and scour the soil. Roots may be laid bare and trees even toppled. The main remedies are:

- to thin the hedge by cutting gaps; careful harvesting of leafy branches for fodder or poles, lopping, pruning, and other management practices outlined in Unit 18 will thin the hedge-windbreak to a density suitable for its purpose.
- to plant a guard row on the windward side and in addition thin the hedge. Two parallel thin, gappy hedges are more efficient than one solid hedge.

Summary of units 15 to 19   Hedges and ditches

1. Fences made of living plants (hedges), are less costly than wire fencing and can themselves be crops yielding firewood, medicine, fruit or fodder.

2. Hedges are best started with cuttings because these are easy to see while the hedge is young and they grow bushier than seedlings. Good hedge plants grow roots into the phreatic zone. Take cuttings from plants that stay green in the dry season. Plant at the start of the rains.

3. If the hedge is started with seedlings, their apical buds (at the stem tip) must be clipped off in order to produce bushy growth. Mark each seedling clearly, weed round it and protect it from birds and rodents.

4. In its second year the hedge must be strengthened by interweaving branches with neighbouring plants. This provides support and fills gaps. Larger gaps can be filled by layering – creating new rooted shoots from the parent bush. Trimming or light clipping will produce bushy growth.

5. In the third year controlled grazing may be used to replace clipping.

6. Larger animals that might force their way through hedges can be stopped by a ditch or 'rough strip' of appropriate design.

7. Wind reduces crop yields by drying the soil and by drying leaf surfaces, thus leaving plants with less water than they need for maximum growth. Strong winds can blow seeds from the ground or damage plants physically, tearing leaves and rubbing fruits.

8. Barriers against wind can take the form of shelterbelts composed of several parallel rows or of single row hedges that include taller trees. A dense wind barrier runs the risk of being blown down and does not shelter crops as efficiently as a porous (gappy) barrier. Well sheltered gardens need less watering than more wind-swept, open gardens.

Bibliography

Insects

Collingwood, E. F. *CDH, Les Principaux Enemis des Cultures Maraichers au Senegal.* Cambarene, Dakar. 1986.

Fabre, J. H. *Bumble Bees and Others.* London 1915. This and any other work by the same author are unparallelled accounts of insect behaviour.

Hill, D. S. *Agricultural Insect Pests of the Tropics and their Control.* Cambridge University Press. 1983.

Pears, P. Sherman, B. *How to Control Fruit and Vegetable Pests.* Henry Doubleday Research Assoc. U.K. 1990.

Chemicals

Stoll, G. *Natural Crop Protection in the Tropics* Agrecol, CTA, Switzerland. 1985.

General

Carson, R. *Silent Spring.* Hamish Hamilton, London. 1963.

Dupriez, H. De Leener, P. *African Gardens and Orchards.* CTA, Terre et Vie, Macmillan. 1989.

Lorentz, A. O. *Knotts Handbook for Vegetable Growers.* Wiley. 1980.

Purseglove, J. W. *Dicotelydons.* 2 vols. Longman, U.K. 1968.

Purseglove, J. W. *Monocotelydons.* 2 vols. Longman, U.K. 1972.

Trees

Rocheleau, D., Weber, F. and Field-Juma, A. *Agro-forestry in Dryland Africa.* ICRAF, Nairobi, 1988.

Weber, F. *Forestry in the Arid Tropics.* Vita, Washington, 1987.

Disease

Hill, D. N., Waller, J. *Pests and Diseases of Tropical Crops.* 2 vols. Longman U.K. 1988.

Weltzein, H. C. *The Use of Composted Materials for Leaf Disease Suppression in Field Crops.* Symposium of Crop Protection in Low Input Agriculture. British Crop Protection Council. London. 1990.

Spray equipment

Hand Operated Sprayers Handbook. British Crop Protection Council. 1989.

Nozzle Selection Handbook. BCPC. 1990.

Technical Literature relating to the CP15 Sprayer of Cooper Pegler Ltd. 1990. Cooper Pegler Spraying Technology, 283 London Road, Burgess Hill, W. Sussex RH15 9QU, U.K.

Communication

Parlato, R., Burns Parlato, M. and Cain, B. J. *Fotonovelas and Comic Books. The Use of Popular Graphic Media in Development.* USAID., Washington. 1980.

Index

Note: page numbers in italics refer to illustrations and diagrams.